BIBLE TRUTHS
UNMASKED

FINIS DAKE

BIBLE TRUTHS UNMASKED

FINIS DAKE

Published by: Dake Publishing, Inc.
P. O. Box 1050
Lawrenceville, GA 30045
Web Site: http://www.dake.com
All rights reserved.

Unless otherwise noted, all Scripture quotations are from the Holy Bible, King James Version.

First Printing

Printed in the United States of America.

ISBN: 1-55829-081-8 (paperback)

01 02 03 04 05   87654321

Table of Contents

CHAPTER 1

HOW TO UNDERSTAND THE BIBLE

We have chosen *Bible Truths Unmasked* as the title of this book, because it is our desire to unmask the many plain, simple, and clearly–stated biblical truths that are unnecessarily hidden from many Christians in every denomination. The devil himself is chiefly responsible for these truths being unknown. He not only blinds the minds of them that believe not (2 Cor. 4:3-4), but he steals the Word of God from the hearts of Christians, lest they should discover the means of complete victory over him—victory that is the heritage of every believer. Satan and his agents are transformed into "angels of light" and "ministers of righteousness" to deceive (2 Cor. 11:13-15). He even uses the best of saints and ministers of churches to propagate fallacies of every kind in order to rob men of the richest blessings of the Gospel of Christ. We propose to uncover many of these truths in the following pages. We promise to provide a wealth of clear Scriptures as we seek to unmask truths that have been hidden for generations—truths that have not been fully experienced by Christians since the days of the apostles.

It's quite possible that you'll be astonished at some of our claims, perhaps arguing at first that such is not the teaching of the Bible. But if you'll be honest and open to what the Scriptures really teach, you will be convinced of these truths—and that they are intended to be experienced by all believers.

This Book Reveals God's Will and Shows:

1. How to read and understand the Bible.
2. How to reap the benefits of the promises of God.
3. How to detect demonic powers and false religions.
4. How to resist the devil and overcome him as well as his fallen angels and demons.
5. How to know when you are being deceived and how to prevent deception.
6. How to detect between manifestations of God and those of evil spirits.
7. How to know the will of God.
8. How to know what sins and bad habits will damn the soul.
9. How to distinguish between carnality and sin.
10. How to have freedom from sin, bad habits and spiritual defeat.
11. How to be born again and know God in reality.
12. How to solve all the problems of life, both now and hereafter.
13. How to have unwavering, unshakable, and absolute faith in God.
14. How to know you have the right faith and the right religion.
15. How to increase faith and how to use it.
16. How to be prosperous and succeed in business.
17. How to know if you will go to Heaven or Hell.
18. How to overcome obstacles to faith and hindrances to prayer.
19. How to have freedom from poverty and want.

20. How to obtain answers to every prayer.
21. How to know when prayer is not going to be answered.
22. How to know when your prayer will be answered.
23. How to know when it is God's will to heal and answer prayer.
24. How to obtain bodily healing and sound health.
25. How to have freedom from sickness, pain, and disease.
26. How to become master of yourself and be free from worry and anxiety.
27. How to do the works of Christ and even greater works than He did.
28. How to have power with God.
29. How to have all the gifts of the Holy Spirit.
30. How to exercise unlimited authority in all the fullness of God.

The Basis of Proof for These Claims

The basis of proof for the claims we've listed is the Bible. There are many books designed to provide a temporary relief from life's problems. Primarily concerned with outward appearance, these books are based upon a mixture of psychology and religion. They are not without merit, but they miss the mark completely when it comes to dealing with the heart of the trouble of the human race—and they certainly provide no permanent cure. The great trouble in our world is not so much outward maladjustment as it is inward depravity caused by sin and rebellion against God. The fact is that men are depraved and fallen creatures and out of harmony with God and His creative purposes. They are dominated by evil spirits who seek to control every act of their life and conduct contrary to the divine will.

If we are to become victorious over the adversities we face and attain the full benefits of the gospel, we must be enlightened as to the true source of our troubles and turn to God for help over these evil spirits that dominate the human race. If we are to have complete and eternal victory, we must find our help in God, through the Truth found in Scripture, and not through psychology and human effort. The Bible must be accepted as the inspired and infallible Word of God. What it says must be accepted as the *final word of authority* on all questions.

The law of the Bible is that in the mouth of two or three witnesses every word shall be established (Mt. 18:16; 2 Cor. 13:1). We propose to follow this law and to prove everything by that which is plainly written in Scripture. It is important that the reader be willing to lay aside any theory that may be contrary to the plain Word of God. Let us accept at face value what God says and refuse to question God or to "make His Word a lie" about anything it says.

God Means What He Says and Says What He Means

When God says something, He means it. We have all the right in the world to believe that He is an intelligent Being and that He can (and does) use the human language as well as any of us. There is nothing to be gained by doubting, questioning, or arguing about everything that He says. We stand to lose everything, both now and hereafter, if we pursue such a program. It is the purpose of the devil to convince men to live in doubt and unbelief concerning the promises of God, so as to rob them of the benefits of faith in His Word. If God did not mean what He said then He should not have said it—but if He did say it, who are we to make Him a liar? Shall we not rather believe that the devil is a liar, that he is our worst enemy, and that doubt and unbelief are his work for the purpose of robbing men of the benefits of the gospel through Jesus Christ?

No Room for Misunderstanding

There can be no excuse for misunderstanding the Bible concerning anything it says. The Bible is the most simple book in the world to understand. We are only required to believe the Bible and accept the truth of the Scriptures. Not one passage in the Bible even hints that it is difficult to understand. It is only the "unlearned and unstable" that are referred to as the ones who wrest the Scriptures to their own destruction (2 Pet. 3:16). It is the "fools, and slow of heart to believe" that misunderstand Scripture (Lk. 24:25-27). It is "unbelief and hardness of heart" that causes men to question what the Bible says (Mt. 13:14-17; Mk. 16:13-14). Men who desire to know the truth can easily understand it if they will make up their minds that what the Bible says is final as far as they are concerned.

The secret of knowing truth is to find out what God says and then believe it. To try and find deep and hidden meanings in what is simple, plain and clear will automatically rob one of a simple faith in God and in His Word. True understanding and faith comes by hearing the Word of God (Rom. 10:11-18). About ninety times in Scripture there is an appeal for men to believe what "is written," as if everything was simple enough to understand if they wanted to believe.

Causes for Misunderstanding

Pride, willful unbelief, doubt, and rebellion against what "is written" are the causes of misunderstanding the Bible. The difficulty is not in understanding what is plainly written, but in being willing to believe and obey it. If one could not understand the truth, he could not reject it. The trouble with the rebels in Matthew 13: 9-11 was not a problem with understanding what had been said, but with rejecting what they had heard. This passage says,

> For this people's heart is waxed gross, and their ears are dull of hearing, and their eyes they have closed; lest at any time they should see with their eyes and hear with their ears, and should understand with their heart, and should be converted, and I should heal them.
> *Matthew 13:9-11 KJV*

We will find any Scripture difficult to understand if we make up our minds that we are not going to believe it. When one rejects what he hears and refuses to obey it, he will naturally be hardened and turned against it. When one closes his mind to truth, there can be no simple understanding of it. We must be willing to accept the

Bible as God's Word. We must believe that God could not be honest if He sought to hide from us the very things He will judge us by in the end. We must accept what the Bible says, not what men interpret it to say. We must believe that God knew what He said and that He meant exactly what He said.

Many Bible References as Proof

It is our policy to provide Scripture references to support everything written between the covers of this book. These passages are given as proof that what we say is biblical, and as an aid for those who desire to investigate for themselves what the Bible has to say. Some of the Scripture we present may contradict what you have been taught in Church. In these cases, be sure that you do not allow preconceived ideas and doctrinal teachings to cause you to be biased. Do not seek to make the Bible conform to your ideas. Conform your ideas to the Bible. Let the plain language of Scripture settle every point of difference and confirm what you believe.

God's Promises are Especially Simple

We've stated that many people think the Bible is hard to understand. In particular, this belief is held by many concerning the prophecies, the proverbs, and some figures of speech. However, these seemingly difficult parts of the Bible are no more difficult to understand than the sections of the Bible that deal with history, or those that many consider to be "simple." Prophecy is nothing more than history written beforehand and should be understood in this light. All riddles, allegories, types, symbols, and figures of speech are either explained in Scripture, or are clear in themselves as to their true meaning.

When it comes to the promises of God, there shouldn't be any misunderstanding about what they say or mean. Every promise of God is a simple statement of obligation to men that God will give them certain benefits when they meet certain conditions. All the promises of God are conditional, as can be seen in the Scriptures themselves. If you want to receive the promised benefits, you must accept the promise for what it says and meet the conditions required. You can then depend upon the fulfillment of God's promise *in this life*. Since God cannot lie, man is assured that what God has promised He is abundantly able to perform. None of God's promises need further interpretation. All that we must do is act upon what the Bible says and believe that God's promise will be fulfilled in our lives. Do not attach any other conditions to God's promises than what is plainly written. When the conditions are met the blessings will be realized. As the Apostle Paul writes in 2 Corinthians 1:20, "For *all* the promises of God in Him are yea, and in Him Amen, unto the glory of God by us."

Chapter Two

THE REALITY OF GOD, SATAN, ANGELS, AND DEMONS

The Reality of the Living God

Faith in God and in His promises presupposes the existence of God and that He is a God of love, justice, mercy and truth. This is a fundamental idea, and one on which this entire book is based. We must acknowledge these characteristics of God, and do so without doubt in our hearts. Paul said, "But without faith it is impossible to please him: for he that cometh to God *must believe that he is*, and *that he is a rewarder* of them that diligently seek him" (Heb. 11:6). You can and should believe in God if you want to recieve any of the benefits from Him that He has promised. We will not take up a complete study of God—that topic is fully dealt with in our book titled, *God's Plan for Man*. Instead, we will proceed with the assumption that you believe in a personal God; that the Bible is the Word of God; and that God will be true to you in all that He has promised. We must build upon this fundamental, biblical foundation, and as you receive the benefits of the promises, you will have the best possible proof of the existence of God and of His faithfulness to His obligations to man.

The Reality of Satan

The Bible not only teaches the reality of a personal God, but also the reality of a personal devil—the adversary of God and man. Satan is mentioned by various names about 175 times in Scripture. Jesus, the apostles, and the Bible writers refer to him as a real person (1 Chr. 21:1; Zech. 3:1-3; Mt. 4:1-11; Eph. 6:10-18; 1 Pet. 5:8-9; Rev. 12:7-12; 20:1-10). Personal pronouns, descriptions, names, attributes, and works are ascribed to Satan in Scripture. He is pictured as the head of the spirit forces who have rebelled against God (Mt. 12:24-30; Eph. 2:2; 6:10-18; 2 Cor. 11:14; Rev. 12:7-12). He is a fallen angel and the former ruler of the planet Earth before the days of Adam. He led a rebellion against God and ascended into Heaven to cast God out. He was defeated and the Earth cursed and all life on the Earth was totally destroyed by the flood of Genesis 1:2; 2 Peter 3:4-7; and Psalm 104:6-9. He was sinless and perfect in his ways from his creation until sin was found in him (Ezek. 28:11-17). He was cast out of Heaven when he was defeated (Isa. 14:12-14; Lk. 10:18). The Earth remained desolate until God restored it in six days and made man and the present creation (Jer. 4:23-26; Gen. 1:2-31).

Satan, therefore, is not a disease germ, an error of the mortal mind, an evil principle, or a being complete with hoofs, horns, a tail and a pitchfork, residing over the realm of Hell. Instead, the Bible reveals Satan as a real person, and his activities and personality are clear:

1. He is the deceiver of all men (Rev. 12:9; 20:1-10; 2 Cor. 11:14).
2. He had the power of death until Christ conquered death, Hell, and the grave (Heb. 2:14; 1 Cor. 15:24-28; Rev. 1:18; 20:11-15).

3. He is the leader of all sinners and backsliders in the human race (1 Jn. 3:8-10; 1 Tim. 5:15) and of all spirit rebels (Eph. 6:10-18; Mt. 9:34).
4. He causes all sickness and disease and physical and mental maladies (Lk. 13:16; Jn. 10:10; Acts 10:38).
5. He takes advantage of the adversities faced by men to further their rebellion and hold them captive (2 Cor. 2: 11; 1 Tim. 1:20; 5:11-15; 1 Pet. 5:8-9).
6. He tempts and provokes men to sin (1 Chr. 21:1; Mk. 1:13; 1 Cor. 7:5).
7. He causes offense and opposition to God (Mt. 16: 23).
8. He transforms himself into an angel of light to deceive (2 Cor. 11:14).
9. He resists others who would serve God (Zech. 3:1-2; 1 Pet. 5:8-9).
10. He enters into union with others against God (Lk. 22:3; Jn. 13:2).
11. He sends messengers to defeat saints (2 Cor. 12:1-7; Dan. 10:12-21).
12. He hinders the gospel (1 Th. 2:18; Acts 13:10).
13. He steals the Word of God from the hearts of the people, lest they should believe it and be saved (Mt. 13:19; Lk. 8:12).
14. He endues men with power to work miracles (2 Th. 2:9; Rev. 13:1-18).
15. He wars on messengers of God and sometimes holds them captive. (Dan. 10:12-21).
16. He sets snares for men to fall into sin (1 Tim. 3:7; 2 Tim. 1:26).
17. He makes war on the saints (Eph. 6:10-18; 1 Pet. 5: 8-9).
18. He causes diversions and blinds men to the gospel (2 Cor. 4:4).

19. He causes "double mindedness" (Jas. 1:5-9); "doubt and unbelief" (Rom. 14:23; Gen. 3:4-5); "darkness and oppression" (2 Cor. 4:4; 2 Pet. 1:4-9); "deadness and weakness" (Heb. 6:1; 9:14); "delay and compromise" (Acts 24:25; 26:28); and "divisions and strife" among men (1 Pet. 5:8; 1 Cor. 3:1-3).

20. He stirs up the passions and lusts of men and gains control of them as they submit to his demonic forces (Jn. 8:44; Eph. 2:1-3; 1 Jn. 2:15-17).

The Reality of Fallen Angels

Angels are real beings with spirit bodies. In fact, the only real difference between angels and the human race is that angels have spiritual bodies and are greater in power and personal attributes. That angels are indeed personal beings is proven by a great number of Scripture references:

1. Angels are intelligent and wise (2 Sam. 14:20; 19:27; Mt. 24:35).

2. They are immortal and mighty (Dan. 10:5-21; Lk. 20:36; Rev. 12:7-12).

3. They are not demons or human beings (Acts 23: 8-9; Heb. 2:9, 16).

4. They have wills and spirit bodies with bodily parts like men (Isa. 14:12-14; Dan. 10:5-21; Rev. 12:7-12; 20:1-10; Gen. 18-19; Josh. 5).

5. They can and do operate in the material realm (Rev. 9:11, 14; 12:7-12; 20:1-10).

6. They wage war in actual bodily combat (Rev. 12: 7-9; Dan. 10:5-21).

7. They rule nations (Dan. 10:13-21; 12:1; Eph. 6:10-18).

8. They are created sons of God (Gen. 6:1-4; Job 1: 6; 2:1; 38:7; Col. 1:15-18).
9. They are organized into principalities and powers to war on saints (Rom. 8:38; Eph. 6:10-18; 1 Pet. 3:22).
10. They are of two classes—good and bad (2 Pet. 2: 4; Jude 6-7; Rev. 12:7-9).
11. They are made subject to Christ (1 Pet. 3:22).
12. Rebelious angels will be cast out of Heaven (Rev. 12:7-12).
13. Fallen angels "deceive men" (2 Cor. 11:14); "oppose saints" (Rom. 8:38; Eph. 6:10-18); "originally fell with Lucifer" (Isa. 14:12-14; Ezek. 28:11-17; Mt. 24:41; Rev. 12:7-12); and "are doomed to eternal Hell" (Mt. 25:41; Jude 6-7; Isa. 24:21-23; 25:7).
14. They "eat food" (Gen. 18; Ps. 78:49); "wear clothes" (Jn. 20:12); "observe men" (1 Cor. 4:9); "cook" (1 Ki. 19:5-7); "travel" (Rev. 8:13; 9:1); "speak languages" (1 Cor. 13:1); "witness confessions" (Lk. 15:8-9); and do many things men do.
15. They have personal soul and spirit faculties like men (Lk. 15:1-10; 1 Cor. 11:10; Mk. 8:38; Lk. 2: 13; Rev. 5:11; Job 4:18).
16. They have made appearances with bodies like men (Gen. 18:1-16; 19:1-5; Josh. 5:15; Judg. 6: 11; 13:6-20; Dan. 10; Acts 12:7-11; Heb. 13:2).

Reality of Demons or Unclean Spirits

Demonic activity is very real, according to the Bible. The word "demon" is not found in Scripture, but it means "evil spirit" or "devil." The word "devil" is used of *Satan*, the prince of demons (Mt. 9:34; 12:24). He is the chief evil spirit and the original source of evil in the universe. The Greek word for "devil" used in conjunction with Satan is *diabolos*, meaning "adversary," "false accuser," or "slanderer." It is translated "false accuser" and "slanderer" and is used of men in 1 Timothy 3:11; 2 Timothy 3:3; and Titus 2:3. It is translated "devil" once when applied to Judas when he became an adversary of Christ (Jn. 6:70). In thirty–four other places it is used of Satan as the chief adversary of God and man and is translated "devil."

Only One Devil, but Many Demons

In the other seventy–six places where the words "devil" and "devils" are found, they refer to evil spirits or demons and the word is derived from two different Greek words—*diamonion* and *diamon*, meaning "evil spirits," "devils," or "adversaries" of God and man. There is only one chief devil, but there are many demons. The devil has an angelic body and cannot enter bodily into anyone, but demons are disembodied spirits and do not seem to be able to function in the material world except through possession of men and beasts who have bodies through which they can operate.

Other Facts About Demons

A. They are called: "devils" (Mk. 16:17); "familiar spirits" (Lev. 20:6); "unclean spirits" (Mk. 1:27); "evil spirits" (Lk. 7:21); and "seducing spirits" (1 Tim. 4:1).

B. Demons are made subject to Christ and believers by the atonement; by the name of Jesus; and by the

Holy Spirit (Mt. 8:16-17; 12:28; Mk. 16:17; Lk. 10:17; Acts 19:15).

C. Thousands of demons can enter into and take possession of one man at the same time (Mk. 5:9).

D. They must be discerned, tested, resisted, and rejected by believers (1 Jn. 4:1-6; 1 Cor. 12:10; Eph. 5:27; 6: 10-18; 1 Pet. 5:8-9).

E. They are possessed of more than ordinary intelligence (Mt. 8:29).

F. The rightful place for demons is in the Abyss (Lk. 8: 31; Rev. 9:1-21).

G. They have separate personalities (Lk. 8:26-33).

H. They are disembodied spirits (Mt. 12:43-45; Rev. 16:13-16).

I. They are Satan's emissaries (Mt. 12:26-29).

J. They are numerous, seeking to enter and control men and beasts (Mk. 5:1-18; Mt. 12:43-45; Lk. 8:32).

K. Demon possession and demonic influence are different (Mt. 4:23-24 with 16:21-23).

L. Demons know their fate to be one of torment (Mt. 8:31-32).

M. They know those who have power over them (Acts 19:13-17).

N. They "fear God" (Jas. 2:19); "make war on saints" (Eph. 6:10-18); and "influence men to commit sin" (1 Tim. 4:1-5; 2 Pet. 2:10-12).

O. All unbelievers are more or less possessed with them (Mt. 12:43-45; Eph. 2:1-3).

P. The only resources against them are prayer, bodily control, and the whole armour of God (Mt. 17:21; Eph. 6:10-18).

Q. Traffic with demon spirits is forbidden in both Testaments (Lev. 19:31; 20:6; Dt. 18:10; Isa. 8:19-

21; 1 Chr. 10:13-14; Lk. 4:41; Acts 16:16; 1 Tim. 4:1-5; 2 Pet. 2:1-3; 1 Jn. 4:1-6).

The Nature of Demons

They are: "evil" (Judg. 9:23; 1 Sam. 18:9-10); "intelligent" and "wise" (1 Tim. 4:1; 1 Ki. 22:22-24; Acts 16:16); "powerful" (Mk. 5:1-18; Rev. 16:13-16); "not angels" (Acts 23:8-9); "not human," for they possess men and can be cast out (Mt. 10:7; Mk. 16:17); and "are individuals" (Mk. 16:9).

They have: "knowledge" (Mt. 9:21; Lk. 4:41; Acts 19: 15); "faith" (Jas. 2:19); "feelings" (Mt. 8:29; Mk. 5:7); "fellowship" (1 Cor. 10:20-21); "doctrines" (1 Tim. 4: 1); "wills" (Mt. 12:43-45); "miraculous powers" (Rev. 16:13-16); "intelligence" (1 Tim. 4:l; 1 Jn. 4:1-6); "emotions" (Acts 8:7); "desires" (Mt. 8:28-31); and other soul and spirit faculties.

The Work of Demons

They possess people and cause: "dumbness" and "deafness" (Mt. 9:32-33; Mk. 9:25); "blindness" (Mt. 12:22); "grievous vexation" (Mt. 15:22); "lunacy and mania" (Mt. 4:23-24; 17:14-21; Mk. 5:1-18); "uncleanness" (they are called "unclean spirits" twenty–one times, Lk. 4:36); "supernatural strength" (Mk. 5:1-18); "suicide" (Mt. 17:15; Jn. 10:10); "fits" (Mk. 9:20); "lusts" (Jn. 8:44; Eph. 2:1-3; 1 Jn. 2:15-17); "counterfeit worship" (Lev. 17:7; Dt. 32:17; 2 Chr. 11:15; Ps. 106:37; 1 Cor. 10:30; Rev. 9:20); "error" (1 Jn. 4:1-6; 1 Tim. 4:1); "sickness and disease" (Mt. 4:23-24; 12:22; 17:15-18; Acts 10:38); "torments" (Mt. 4:23-24; 15:22); "deceptions" (1 Tim. 4:1-2; 1 Jn. 4:1-6); "lying" (1 Ki.

22:21-24); "enchantments and witchcraft" (1 Sam. 28; 1 Chr. 10:13; 2 Chr. 33:6); "heresies and false doctrines" (1 Tim. 4:1); "wickedness" (Lk. 11:26); "fear" (2 Tim. 1:7); "worldliness" (1 Jn. 2:15-17; 1 Cor. 2:12); "bondage" (Rom. 8:15); "discord" (Mt. 13:39; 1 Ki. 22:21-24); "violence" (Mt. 17:15); "betrayals" (Jn. 13:2; 1 Ki. 22:22-23); "oppression" (Acts 10:38); "sin" (1 Jn. 3:8); "persecution" (Rev. 2:10; 1 Pet. 5:8); "jealousy" (1 Sam. 16:17; 18:8-10); "false prophecy" (1 Sam. 18:8-10; 1 Ki. 22:21-24); and cause every evil they possibly can to come to God and man.

They can: "teach" (1 Tim. 4:1); "steal" (Mt. 13:19; Lk. 8:12); "fight" (Eph. 4:27; 6:10-18; 1 Pet. 5:8); "get mad" (Mt. 8:28; Rev. 12:12); "tell fortunes" (Lev. 20:27; Acts 16:16); "be friendly" (called "familiar spirits" sixteen times, Lev. 20:6, 27); can go out and come back into men as they will, unless cast out and rejected (Mt. 12:43-45); "travel" (1 Ki. 22:21-24; Mk. 5:7, 12); "speak" (Mk. 1:34; 5:12; Acts 8:7); "imitate departed dead" (1 Sam. 28:3-9; 1 Chr. 10:13; Isa. 8:19; Dt. 18:11); and do a great many other things when in possession of bodies through which they operate.

Demons and Disease Germs

There are demonic spirits for every sickness, unholy trait, and doctrinal error found in the world today. Demons must be cast out in order to obtain relief from their influence. Disease germs, which are closely allied with unclean spirits, are really living forms of corruption which enter into our bodies, causing sickness and death. Just as refuse breeds maggots, so man in his fallen state of corruption breeds germs through unclean living and through contact with corruptions in the fallen world. Germs are agents of Satan, corrupting the bodies of his victims through unclean spirits that work unseen among us.

Knowledge about Demons Necessary

One must believe in the reality of Satan, fallen angels, and demons before he can intelligently cooperate with God against them and resist them in his own life. They are real, and the fact that they deceive men into thinking they are non–existent all the more proves their reality. If we want the benefits of God according to the gospel, then we must believe what God has said about these beings and how they work to bring about sin, sickness, pain, suffering, poverty, want, and defeat, leading many to eternal Hell in the end.

Chapter Three

THE REALITY OF SPIRITUAL WARFARE

Satan the World Deceiver
(Rev. 12:9)

The greatest and most important work of Satan is to counterfeit the doctrines and experiences of God as revealed in Scripture in order to deceive the saints. We are commanded to test every doctrine and supernatural experience to see if they are from God or from Satan (1 Cor. 2:12-16; Phil. 1:9-10; 1 Th. 5:21-22; 1 Jn. 4:1-6). Due to the diversity among the world's religions, their doctrines and individual experiences among their adherents, it is obvious that they cannot all have godly origins. Therefore, we must judge between them by gaining a clear understanding of the clearly–written Word of God. The greatest danger for Christians is to unquestioningly accept everything in the realm of the supernatural as originating with God. Having consecrated themselves to yield to the Holy Spirit and to the leadings of God, believers often think that they cannot be deceived or led astray by evil spirits through counterfeit doctrines and readings. But the fact that a believer is a child of God does not stop the devil from trying, in every conceivable way, to imitate God. In fact, believers are precisely the ones on whom he concentrates his greatest efforts and against whom he wages war.

Latter Day Deceptions and Satanic Powers Predicted

Just as the magicians in Egypt imitated God's power in the days of Moses (Ex. 7:9–8:19), the devil is seeking to counterfeit the true work and plan of God for man in these latter days. In many religious cults there are manifestations of satanic power in the areas of healing and prosperity. Often the adherents of these cults receive benefits similar to those that God has promised for His children. Jesus predicted that in the last days many false Christs and prophets would come who would "shew great signs and wonders; inasmuch that, if it were possible, they shall deceive the very elect" (Mt. 7:22-23; 24:24).

Paul predicted the same thing when he wrote, "Now the Spirit speaketh expressly, that in the latter times some shall depart from the faith, giving heed to seducing spirits and doctrines of devils" (1 Tim. 4:1-8; 2 Tim. 3:1-13; 4:1-4). He also predicted that the future Antichrist is:

> . . . coming after the working of Satan with all power and signs and lying wonders, and with all deceivableness of unrighteousness in them that perish; because they received not the love of the truth, that they might be saved. And for this cause God shall send them strong delusions

that they should believe a lie; that they
might be damned who believed not the
truth, but had pleasure in unrighteousness
                    2 Thessalonians 2:8-12

Peter and John also predicted that Satan would grant a
great degree of power to men in the last days (2 Pet. 2:
1-3; Rev. 13:1-18; 19:20).

Two Sources of Supernatural Help

Thus, we can see that many will seek and find help
from satanic powers in the last days. Satan and demons
who cause disease, who hinder men from obtaining
prosperity, and who fight to prevent men from receiving
answers to their prayers, can also withdraw this opposition and provide help to obtain these benefits, should
circumstances be favorable to them.

Satan and demons can not only aid men, but they
can hold them in physical, spiritual and material bondage and defeat, until they come to know the truth that
sets them free. God alone can deliver from their power,
unless of their own accord these demonic influences
relinquish their hold. Jesus taught in Matthew 12:43-
45 that demons can leave a person and then come back
again if they desire. The fact that they flee when rebuked
by those who have power over them proves that they can
loose any person they bind (Mt. 12:22-32; Lk. 10:18-20;
Acts 19:11-17). It stands to reason that if they can inflict
disease, they can also remove disease when it is to their
advantage to do so.

When would demonic powers find it advantageous

to remove diseases that they themselves have inflicted? The answer to this question lies in the motivations and schemes of the enemy. Satan and his followers use the deception of false doctrines that deny the essentials of the gospel of salvation. The deceived followers of these false religions never come to know the true source of their power. They may be convinced that the source of their wealth, health and power must be God, but this is not true. Jesus said that in the judgment "Many will say unto me . . . Lord, Lord, have we not prophesied in thy name? and in thy name cast out devils? and in thy name done many wonderful works? And then will I profess unto them, *I never knew you: depart from me, ye that work iniquity*" (Mt. 7:21-23).

These false religions, without exception, deny the blood of Christ, the new birth, the bodily resurrection of Jesus, and all the essentials of the Gospel that save the souls of men. The devil reinforces such teaching by helping those who follow these religions, convincing them that they have at last found truth. However, they ignore Christianity and the truth of God's Word, and will be damned in the end because they have rejected Jesus Christ and the Cross (Acts 4:12).

God is the true source of help, not the devil and demons. We come to you with the true message of the Bible, and we guarantee upon the authority of the Word of God that you will find healing, health, prosperity, answers to your prayers, and everything that God promises you. You can know God in a real and vital way, and enjoy the fullness of God in your life as you walk in truth and conform to the will of God. Then, too, your eternal soul will be saved in the end, and you will have eternal life instead of eternal damnation, which the followers of these false religions will have to endure.

We want it clearly understood that there are two sources of help, but if you will let the true God be your source of help, you will receive God's blessings in this life as well as in the life to come.

How Satan Deceives the World

Paul said, "And no marvel; for Satan himself is transformed into an angel of light. Therefore, it is no great thing if his ministers also be transformed as the ministers of righteousness; whose end shall be according to their works" (2 Cor. 11:14-15). This makes it clear that counterfeits of Satan in doctrines and manifestations will be substitutes of truth and as near to the light and truth as possible in order to deceive those who seek after truth. Thus, it is imperative that we be careful about what we choose to believe and the supernatural power to which we yield. There are definite methods outlined in Scripture by which one can detect the type of spirit which may be seeking control.

How to Detect Counterfeit Religions and Demon Workings

(1) *Any doctrine that denies or in any way causes doubt and unbelief concerning anything taught in Scripture has demonic origins.* Any religion that denies the inspiration of the Bible; the reality of God as a person; the divine sonship of Jesus Christ as the only begotten

Son of God; the virgin birth; the pre–existence of Jesus Christ; the divinity of Christ and His miraculous power and supernatural ministry; the death, burial, bodily resurrection, and the bodily manifestation of Christ after His resurrection; the bodily ascension to Heaven and the coming again of Jesus Christ to set up a kingdom in the world forever; the reality and power of the Holy Spirit and His ministry to convict of sin, to create men in Christ, and to carry on the work of God among men; the reality of the Christian experience including the new birth, cleansing from sin, living free from sin, divine healing, the Spirit baptism, gifts of the Spirit, miracles, and signs following believers, answers to prayer, fulfillment of the promises in obtaining health, happiness, prosperity, and the numerous other experiences of the New Testament; the reality of Satan, demons, sickness, sin, and the fall of man; the creation of all things by God; the free moral agency of men; the universality of sin and the depravity of man; the necessity of repentance and the born again experience; the eternal loss of the soul as the penalty for sin; the necessity of the atonement; the reality of Heaven and eternal Hell; the resurrection and judgment of all men; and the immortality of the soul is not of God. Any religion that teaches contrary to these and all other fundamental doctrines of Scripture is of the devil and exists for the purpose of causing the soul to be damned in eternal Hell.

(2) *Any power, influence, or doctrine that causes one to become passive, inactive, submissive, and unresisting to the workings of supernatural spirits which seek to control the life contrary to Scripture, is not of God.* God's Spirit always, and without exception, wants free and active choice in the surrender of the will as it gets

light according to the Scriptures. God seeks intelligent action, while demons demand the surrender of the will without active choice to do as one intelligently sees fit. They demand passivity on the part of their victims. They demand that man be a mere machine, an automaton, and that he be submissive to them. They seek absolute control and compulsory action through men.

When one asserts that a spirit is making demands and forcing compliance to those demands, it is a sure sign that one is being moved by the wrong spirit. Demons work to motivate men to act quickly and unintelligently—leading them to these actions regardless of the outcome to the cause of Christ and lost souls. The spirits of Christians are always subject to them, and anything that demands a lack of control over the individual's personal spirit is the wrong spirit (1 Cor. 14:32). The Holy Spirit never causes people to act indecently and disorderly, to call attention to self in public services, or do things which they never would do in private.

Causes of Passivity and Defeat Among Christians

(1) A determination to obey the supernatural, thinking that surrender is a guarantee against demon operation.

(2) A desire to have communication with God leads them to believe that all supernatural influences and spirits must be of God, so many times they yield to the wrong spirit or accept the wrong doctrine.

(3) A deep hunger to be wholly surrendered to God and to be submissive to Him in all things leads them to

submit, subdue, and make all things subject to the supernatural, so they unconsciously accept demonic workings and are deceived.

(4) A lack of knowledge of the workings of demonic powers and of the readings and guidance of God, consequently there is failure at times to distinguish between good and evil influences.

(5) Ignorance of the Bible and wrong interpretation of Scriptures that deal with demons and their manifestations.

(6) Blind yieldedness to any and all spirit workings regardless of the source (so often they yield to the wrong spirit).

(7) Ignorance of the true workings of the Holy Spirit according to the Scriptures.

(8) Promises to obey God's Word, but following the wrong spirit.

(9) A longing to know God and His spiritual operations makes them anxious and quick to yield to counterfeit workings of God by evil spirits.

(10) A desire to be used of God in order to prove their contact with the supernatural power promised to all men.

Ignorance No Guarantee Against Demons

One must realize that ignorance is no guarantee against the workings of evil spirits. In fact, this is one of the chief means by which these spirits gain control. If they can move anyone to accept their suggestions, doctrines, ideas, readings, and guidance, they won't be satisfied, but will be tireless in their attempts to gain even more ground. In order to work through a man demons must keep him in ignorance of the truth. Paul warned believers not to "give place to the devil" (Eph. 4:27) and to "put on the whole armour of God, that ye may be able to stand against the wiles of the devil . . . to quench all the fiery darts of the wicked" (Eph. 6:10-18). When a person becomes contentious over doctrines not plainly stated in Scripture, or doctrines that are contrary to Scripture, he is a victim of demonic possession and demonic teaching. A person under the control of the Holy Spirit will be gentle, humble, honest, and open–minded to truth. He will be eager to accept as truth what is shown him to be plainly written in the Word of God. He will not be stubborn to hold on to personal ideas or to prove that he is right in total disregard of what the Bible says. He will be ready and willing to accept new truth and to walk in the light as he receives it (1 Jn. 1:7).

How to Keep from Being Deceived

When someone is born again and becomes a spiritual person, that person enters into the realm of the supernatural and spiritual. He should begin his new life with a study of the Bible to see what it teaches and how he should walk and how to conduct spiritual warfare. If he neglects to be on guard and fails to be aggressive against satanic powers, he is liable to be defeated by them. There is nothing to be afraid of if one lives a conscientious Christian life by reading the Bible and praying daily and by living in the Spirit according to light received from God's Word (Col. 2:6-8; Gal. 5:16-26; Rom. 8: 1-13; 1 Jn. 1:7). One should get up every morning and pray and have faith in God's help through the day. He should always meditate on the Scriptures and refuse to do anything that might be contrary to the known will of God as the Bible teaches and there will be no danger of being deceived.

We must learn not to believe anything concerning spiritual and eternal things unless it is explicitly stated in Scripture or is in harmony with them. It matters not if it comes from the best ministers in the land or from an angel from Heaven. It should be judged by what the Bible says before it is accepted as truth. We must learn to judge every impression, revelation, dream, vision or sermon. The possibility of deception should keep everyone on guard and open to testing everything by the Bible (2 Tim. 2:15; 3:15-17).

How to Detect the Manifestations of the Holy Spirit

The true manifestation of the Holy Spirit will be earmarked by the following clear–cut rules and Christian principles:

(1) A Christ–like spirit of love, patience, and faith in God (Gal. 5:21-22).
(2) Soberness and keenness of spirit vision (2 Tim. 1:7; 1 Cor.12:1-11).
(3) Deep humility of heart and meekness of spirit, with lion–like courage against sin, sickness, poverty, disease, discouragement, failure, and every other thing that could cause defeat in the Christian life (Acts 1: 8; 10:38; Rom. 8:1-13; Gal. 5:16-26).
(4) Absolute clearness of the mental faculties in intelligent action to carry out Bible instructions concern-

ing known duty and personal life as a Christian (1 Cor. 14:32; 2 Tim. 1:7).

(5) Freedom from all fault–finding, surmising, whispering, or slander to anyone, and freedom from all the works of the flesh that are listed in Rom. 1:29-32; 1 Cor. 6:9-11; Gal. 5:19-21; Mk. 7:19-21.

(6) The lack of a condemning and judging spirit, or a desire to hurt anyone by thought, word or deed. All should be done for the edification and betterment of all concerned and in accord with the golden rule (1 Cor. 13; Eph. 4:22-32; 5:1-18).

(7) Freedom from ignorance concerning the divine will at the moment. When one is moved upon to act quickly and urgently without knowing whether the act will glorify God or not, it will be best to wait and pray until it is clear beyond all doubt that God wants such action. If it is God who is moving a person to action, it will not insult Him to try the spirit and intelligently judge whether the proposed act is biblical or not, for God commands this kind of judgment on our part (1 Jn. 4:1-6). If it is God, the individual can wait until he is assured by God before he acts. He should wait like Gideon of old, who sought two impossible signs before he knew and acted upon the will of God. However, one must not be guided entirely by so–called fleeces (or the random opening of the Bible for some verse to show God's will). He must judge all "fleeces" by the Word of God and wait until he knows it is God asking him to do something. All acts of God will be primarily for the liberation of men from sin, for the deliverance of the body from pain, sickness, and want, or for some other good thing that someone needs to have done

for him (Acts 10:38). The work of the devil tends to blind, cause sin, discouragement, lack of faith, and failure (Jn. 10:10).

Grounds for the Working of God and Satan

Just as the devil requires lies in the minds of men to hold them in bondage, so God requires truth in the mind for the true working of the Holy Spirit (Jn. 8:31-36). Demonic forces will place hinderances in the way of those seeking the truth (Mt. 13:19; 2 Cor. 4:1-4).

The Duty of Saints in Spiritual Warfare

(1) Beware of neglecting those things that will cause enlightenment in spiritual warfare (Ps. 1:2-4; 2 Tim. 2:15; 3:15-17).
(2) Do not fall an easy prey to the criticism of others or to the pressing cares of life which will keep you occupied from taking time to wage war successfully (Lk. 21:34-36; Eph. 6:10-18).
(3) Do not forget that spiritual weapons alone will give you the victory over sin and Satan (2 Cor. 10:4-7; Eph. 6:10-18).
(4) Do not neglect prayer and reading the Bible (Eph. 6: 18; 1 Tim. 4:12-16).
(5) Do not be discouraged when the conflict for the moment seems to be going against you (1 Tim. 6:12; 2 Tim. 4:7; 1 Pet. 1:7; 4:12; Jas. 1:12).
(6) Be alert and resist Satan (Jas. 4:7; 1 Pet. 5:8-9).
(7) Do not fail to use the authority of Christ through

His precious blood, His name, and the Holy Spirit against evil powers (Acts 1:8; Jn. 14:12-15; Mk. 16:15-20).

(8) Do not fail to do the whole will of God intelligently as it becomes known. Walk in the light of the Word of God (1 Jn. 1:7).

How to Tell When One is Deceived

We are deceived when we think that sin will not have any effect upon us or that we will inherit the kingdom of God regardless of sin in our lives (1 Cor. 6:9-11; Rom. 8:12-13; Gal. 5:19-21). Further, we are deceived when we believe that we will not reap what is sown (Gal. 6:7-8); that it is not necessary to obey the Bible (Jas. 1:22; 2:10); and that we cannot be deceived (1 Cor. 10:12-13; 2 Cor. 11:3-15; 1 Tim. 4:1-9; Eph. 6:10-18). These are all sure marks of demonic deception and delusion.

Many latter–day delusions can be traced back to the fallacies listed above or to a crisis in the lives of the founders of the new religions. They threw themselves open to the supernatural and accepted demonic doctrines and powers instead of judging what they received by the standard of God's Word. No one should blindly obey any spirit or believe any doctrine. Satan has no principle of righteousness and he will take advantage of an honest heart if permitted, as quickly as of a dishonest one.

A Warning to New Believers

Until a new believer becomes acquainted with the Scriptures and the spiritual realm into which he enters upon finding God, he should walk very carefully in prayer and read the Bible for more truth to obey. He must not permit anything to side–track him. If he falls, he must get up and rededicate himself to God and go on more aggressively against his foe than ever before. As we begin learning to distinguish truth from error, very few can guarantee that they are obeying God in every detail, because there are many factors likely to intervene, such as the mind, spirit, will, desires, imaginations, imperfect knowledge and submissiveness, false ideas, and personal feelings, as well as the numerous deceptive intrusions of evil spirits.

The beginner must learn to discern false spirits as well as false doctrines. Deliverance from believing lies occurs by believing truth. Nothing can remove a lie but truth. Nothing can give complete victory over evil but God through the precious blood of Christ and by prayer and constant walking in the Spirit (Rom. 8:1-16; Gal. 5:16-26; Eph. 6:10-18). (For a complete study of divine and satanic workings see our fifty–two lesson Bible course, *God's Plan for Man*).

In the next few chapters we shall deal with the work of demons, showing how men are deceived and held in bondage to Satan through sin and false doctrine.

Chapter Four

MORAL LAW AND MORAL GOVERNMENT

The doctrine of moral law and moral government must be clear if one wants to obtain a proper understanding of sin and its evil effects on man. The following study will enable the reader to see that God rules the universe and that man is responsible to Him for his life and conduct.

Definition of Law

Law is a rule of action established by recognized authority to enforce justice and prescribe duties and obligations to those governed. *Physical law* is the rule of action of the material universe whereby all things are kept perpetually in their own courses, working in harmony according to the divine plan. *Moral law* is the rule of action for free moral agents, directing them in their moral action and their own creative powers according to the divine plan. It is the rule of free and intelligent action and liberty as opposed to the law of bondage and unintelligent action.

The Purpose of Moral Law

The purpose of moral law is to reveal and declare the rule of moral action of free wills concerning the highest good of being and of the universe; and to govern the acts and intents of free wills in their relation to God and the universe. It lies in the reason and declares that which a moral agent ought to choose, will, and intend.

The Immutability of Moral Law

The moral law can never change or vary in its requirement that every being created with a free will consecrate themselves to the same end to which God is consecrated— the highest good of the universe and all things therein. The rebellion of those having free will will never change God's plan concerning the good of His creation. Because of this, moral law can never change.

The Obligation of Moral Law

Because the moral law governs the best good of being, it is naturally obligatory upon all. What is contrary to the good of being is plainly illegal and unwise and must be prohibited. Free moral agents must cooperate to bring about the greatest public good. They must be against that which brings misery and hardships to society. It is a mutual plan for the good of each person and of the universe as a whole, and all are obligated to keep the moral law on every occasion according to the light received.

The Requirement of Moral Government

In order to have moral law there must also be a moral government to direct, guide, and control those having free will. It must include rewards for good and punishments for evil, or no society can function. There must be in every community some standard of living to which all must conform to prove themselves worthy of being part of that society. There must be some means of dealing with rebels who disturb such society. Law without penalties and rewards is no law at all. It is merely advice which can be freely accepted or rejected without fear of punishment or hope of reward. Moral government is under obligation to execute faithfully the moral law.

Requirement of a Moral Governor

Since it is necessary to have a moral law and a moral government to execute this law, there must also be a moral governor whose will and decisions are considered infallible by the subjects of government. This moral governor should be authoritative, not merely advisory. He must be able to maintain the respect of his subjects by faithful and unselfish execution of his duties. He must be able to execute penalties and mete out rewards. Naturally, the one whose attributes and character best qualify him to rule and secure the highest good of all should be the one to rule. It is both his right and duty to be the one to rule. There can be no other person to meet these requirements but God. His natural attributes, His perfect moral character, His relation to the universe as creator and upholder of all things, and His history of absolute justice to all qualify Him to be the Supreme Moral Governor. As our good and His glory depend upon mutual conformity to the same end, He is under obligation to require of us to be holy and consecrated to help Him secure the highest good of being for everyone.

Thus, holiness of life and conduct is a natural obligation to all alike for the best good of all creation.

Free Moral Agency Defined

Free Moral Agency consists of intellect, sensibility, and free will, and these form the foundation of moral obligation to moral government. The intellect includes reason and self–determination. The sensibility includes self–consciousness, sensation, desire, emotion, passion, and all feeling. Free will is the power of choice concerning moral law. It is man's faculty of choosing good or evil without compulsion or necessity. It was originally created in man, and he will have it throughout all eternity.

Biblical Proof That Men are Free Moral Agents

The fact that all men make moral choices and have free choice of action concerning right and wrong proves they are free moral agents. The fact that all men choose freely whether to serve God or Satan, to obey or disobey laws, to choose holiness and salvation or to reject it, proves they have the power of choice. All men of sound mind know they have the power of free choice concerning moral actions. Even if men are bound by sin and Satan they are free to turn to God and find full deliverance—thereafter living for God and the best good of all creation. They are also free to return to sin again if they so choose (Rom. 6:16-23; 8:1-13). No man can deny the fact of free action in normal daily life without incurring the charge of insanity. Men, for the sake of proving some biased church doctrine, may deny the reality of free moral agency—they may even deny their very existence—but the fact remains that they know both.

The Bible declares that all men have the power of free choice and that God is limited in blessing them according to their free cooperation with Him (Jn. 3:15-20, 36; 5:40; 7:17; 9:31; 12:36; 1 Cor. 7:37; 9:17; 1 Pet. 5:2; Mk. 3:35; 16:16; 1 Tim. 2:4; 2 Pet. 3:9; Rev. 22:17; Josh. 24:15; Pr. 1:29-33; Ps. 119:3, 173; Isa. 66:3; Mt. 6:24; etc.).

Every one of these and many other Scriptures plainly state that men are free to choose whom they should serve; that they are responsible for their destiny; that whoever meets the conditions of salvation will be saved and whoever does not will be lost; that God wills for all men to be saved, but if men do not will to be saved they will be lost; that God will judge all men on the basis of their own free choice in accepting or rejecting the gospel; that if it were left up to God's choice and will all men would be saved; and that all men have absolute freedom of choice.

That we have been created with free will is illustrated most clearly in the freedom of men to choose either sin or righteousness—to accept or reject Christ's offer of salvation. If we can exercise our will regarding moral choices, then we are free moral agents. This aspect of God's character with which we are created has far–reaching implications. It is clear from God's Word that those in bondage to sin and demonic powers—even to the point of almost total helplessness—still retain the power of choice. Those in bondage choose to remain in that condition, and they can make the choice to turn from sin and find deliverance in

Jesus Christ. Born in bondage to sin, we have Jesus' promise of deliverance when we turn to God.

Without this God–given power to turn from sin it might be argued that we are not free moral agents. For example, the fact that the Axis nations were overcome by the Allies during World War II is not proof that they did not have the ability to make a free choice. It only proves that the Allies were the stronger of two sets of free moral agents. Their resistance as well as their choice to make war and later to surrender proves they had the power both to will and to act freely. To argue that men do not have the power to choose between right and wrong is to be ignorant of the truth—or it demonstrates willful rebellion against what is clear to all.

The Basis of Right Choice

The obligation to always act for the highest good is the basis of moral action. Every circumstance we encounter is the result of choice—choices we've made or those made by others. It is important that the choices we make have an impact for the greatest public and private good. This moral obligation extends to the ultimate acts of the will or the intention. The moral agent is under obligation to choose holiness as the means to the best good and happiness of being.

The Basis of Justice

Judgment based on intention is the basis of justice under moral government. We also find that this is the basis of justice in civil governments. Whether good intentions lead to bad results, or bad intentions lead to good results, the one making the choice should be held responsible for their intentions and should not be judged on the basis of the results or consequences of their actions. The Bible respects the intention more than the results of outward actions (2 Cor. 8:12; Jas. 1:13-15; 3:9-14). Both vice and virtue are considered to come from the heart (Mk. 7:15-23). Where the heart is right, everything else is considered right, and where the heart is bad, all is considered bad (Mt. 7:15-21). Even sinners do some things outwardly that are required by God, but their hearts are not right. Their intentions are generally selfish, and the acts themselves do not change the heart. Virtue consists of consecration to the same end to which God is consecrated. Vice consists in consecration to the end to which Satan is consecrated—self–gratification contrary to both the moral law and the highest good of the universe.

The Extent of Obedience to the Moral Law

The foundation of moral obligation is our consecration to the highest good of all. Since this is true, then the complete consecration of free wills to secure this end must constitute obedience to moral law. Obedience must be whole and entire. One cannot choose the good of others and at the same time choose self–gratification. God cannot tolerate half–heartedness in choice and service (Rev. 3:15-16; Mt. 22:36-40). He cannot justify one who renders partial obedience. If a person is always falling short of full obedience to his known duty, then he is living under the curse of a broken law (Gal. 3:10-14; Jas. 2: 10; 4:17). God cannot dispense with the execution of the penalty until repentance, forgiveness, and full obedience are realized (Rom. 8:1-13; Gal. 5:16-26; Rom. 6:16-23; Jn. 8:34; 1 Jn. 3:8-10).

Of What Does Disobedience to the Moral Law Consist?

Disobedience to the Moral Law consists of the willing pursuit of self–gratification as the end in life instead of the greatest good of the universe. It consists of the commitment of the will and the consecration of the life to serve sin, Satan and the senses instead of the Moral Law. It seeks to be governed by the impulses and passions instead of intelligence and reason. Self–gratification is the root of all sin. Man's selfishness is closely allied to the self–interests of Satan. The will is always free to oppose desire and lust; but when it does not, sin is committed. The mind knows its obligation, so when it chooses that which is contrary to the law, it is not a choice of ignorance. It becomes a free action and brings condemnation by the law.

Selfishness is always unreasonable. It is the denial of both true manhood and rational nature. It is contempt of the law of God in man's reason. No sinner chooses the way of reason and common sense. In fact, he seldom consults reason for any of his actions. He usually obeys lust and is in a position of stubborn rebellion against reason and the Moral Law. He is lustful at heart whether or not he is able to pursue every lust. As long as he remains so, he is condemned before God and needs the power of regeneration to bring him to obedience to the Moral Law.

The Basis of Degrees of Guilt and Virtue

Both reason and revelation affirm that there are degrees of guilt and virtue; that some are more guilty or more virtuous than others; and that one may be more guilty or more virtuous at one time than at another, whether he is a saint or a sinner. All guilt and virtue are dependent on the exercise of moral obligation, and this depends upon the light and knowledge concerning moral law. Degrees of guilt and virtue are measured by the knowledge of the value of the end chosen in life. The sinner's guilt is equal to his knowledge of the value of the interests he rejects. He is held more responsible today than of old, because he knows more (Acts 17:30; Jas. 4:17). A man's guilt or virtue then, is equal to the knowledge he has of the subject and his conformity to it (Rom. 2:12-16; Jn. 9:41; 15:22-24; Mt. 13:11-12; Lk. 12:47-48).

Selfishness is the rejection of all moral obligation, regardless of light. Sin lies in the intention, and this can be measured only by the knowledge under which the intention is formed and maintained. Thus, if a selfish man should preach the gospel, it would be for the reason that it is the most gratifying thing he could do for himself. He might even preach for the good of others and yet have personal gain as his chief motivation. Take away personal gain—financially or socially—and he would cease to preach. If the same man became a robber, it would be to the same end; not necessarily to do evil, but to gratify self.

If a sinner abstains from evil for the sake of loved ones, his reputation, for fear of judgment or disgrace, or for any reason, it is not because he is good at heart, or because he thinks it is wicked to do that thing, but merely for selfish reasons and personal gain. So it is with every phase of life in which the heart is not right. Natural man looks for gain or advantage in everything. It is only when the sinner consecrates himself to the end of the highest good of being that he ceases being a sinner by nature and practice, and begins to do things from unselfish motivations instead of for self–gratification.

Chapter Five

THE DOCTRINE OF SIN

The Definition of Sin

The Bible plainly states that man is a fallen creature and is in a state of rebellion against God. The Hebrew and Greek words translated "transgression" mean "moral, religious, and national rebellion," "revolt," "unrighteousness," "wickedness," "violation," and "breaking the law."

Sin is twofold:

(1) *The first category is "outward" sin, as we see in the following Scriptures:* "Sin is transgression of the law" (1 Jn. 3:4); "Where no law is, there is no transgression" (Rom. 4:15); "By the law is the knowledge of sin" (Rom 3:20; 7:7); "Sin is not imputed when there is no law" (Rom. 5:13); "All unrighteousness is sin" (1 Jn. 5:17); "Whatsoever is not of faith is sin" (Rom. 14:23); "If ye have respect of persons, ye commit sin" (Jas. 2:9); "The thought of foolishness is sin" (Pr. 24:9; 2 Cor. 10:4-5); "Every idle word that men shall speak" is sin (Mt. 12:36-37); "He that knoweth to do good, and doeth it not, to him it is sin" (Jas. 4:17; Mt. 23:23). These passages teach that all acts, desires, and lusts that cause us to break the laws of God are sin.

(2) *The second category can be described as "inward" sin, as proved by the following passages:* "Ye are of your father the devil, and the lusts of your father ye will do" (Jn. 8:44); "Wherein in time past ye walked according to the course of this world, according to *the prince of the power of the air, the spirit that now worketh in the children of disobedience* . . . fulfilling the desires of the flesh and of the mind; and *were by nature* the children of wrath, even as others" (Eph. 2:1-3); "He that committeth sin is *of the devil*" (1 Jn. 3:8).

These passages and many others prove that sin is something more than mere outward transgression of the law. There is a sin principle, a real nature and spirit of sin, which is the spirit and nature of the devil, that is working in every sinner. This spirit of sin works in man to get him to live contrary to the law of God and the highest good of his own being and of the universe. This spirit and nature of the devil working in men is called "the old man" (Rom. 6:6-12; Eph. 4:22-24; Col. 3:5-15); "the lusts of the flesh" (Eph. 2:3; Gal. 5:19; 1 Jn. 2:15-17); "the body of this death" (Rom. 7:24); "the lusts of sin" (Rom. 6:11-12); "the law of sin and death" (Rom. 7:7-25; 8:2); "the carnal mind" (Rom. 8:1-13); "the power of Satan" (Acts 26:18); "the god of this world" (2 Cor. 4:4); and various other names.

Inbred sin or "the old man" is the spirit and nature of the devil working in men of disobedience. The "old man" is the opposite of righteousness or "the new man" which is the Spirit and nature of God working in men of obedience (Eph. 2:1-3; 4:22-24). The "old man" then is not some part of the body, soul, or spirit of man, but is the spirit and nature of the devil working in man the lusts of sin. The "old man" could be spelled D–E–V–I–L or S–A–T–A–N, and this will express the truth about inbred sin as taught in Scripture.

God is Not the Author of Sin

God is not the author of sin. He warned sinless man against it before he fell (Gen. 2:17). Sin entered the world from an outside source through the malice of the devil (Rom. 5:12-21). Sin originated with Satan when he decided by his own power of choice to rebel against God (Isa. 14:12-14). Others chose to rebel with him and thus, by free choice, transgression of the law of God became a reality. When man chose to transgress the law of God he became sinful (Gen. 2:17; Rom. 5:12-21). Since then the devil and rebellious evil spirits have taken advantage of man's weakness to resist them, controlling the human race. Before the fall man had power over the devil and every form of evil, but when man became sinful the stronger set of rebels—the spirit beings under Satan's rule—became masters of man and his realm. Man can only obtain power over these spirits again through Jesus Christ and the Gospel (Mk. 16:17-18; Jn. 1:12).

The Universal Effect of Sin

The sin of Adam had a universal effect—the imposition of guilt upon all mankind. All men were "in" Adam when he sinned and therefore he could only produce sinful offspring. He was our head and representative and what he did was passed upon all men who were represented by him (Rom. 5:12-21). Just as his blessings would have passed upon all men if he had not sinned, so the effects of the curse are passed upon all men because of his sin. Men now are not personally responsible for Adam's sin, but they are responsible for choosing to remain in sin, following the way of Adam (Jn. 3:16). Each of us can renounce sin and get out from under its dominion and curse by accepting Jesus Christ as our personal Saviour and by consecrating ourselves to obey God (Rom. 6).

All Men are Sinful and Depraved

The present state of those outside of Christ is one of utter depravity—man without God is polluted and corrupt in all his nature. "His understanding is darkened" (Eph. 2:3; 4:18); "his conscience defiled" (Heb. 10:22); "his will obstinate and rebellious" (Rom. 8:7); "his affections carnal and sensual" (Eph. 2:1-3; Gal. 5:19-21; Mk. 7:19-21; Rom. 1:18-32; 1 Cor. 6:9-11); "his thoughts evil continually" (Gen. 6:5; 2 Cor. 10:4-5); "his heart full of abominations" (Jer. 17:9; Mk. 7:19-21; Rom. 1:18-32); and "his life and conduct devoted to living in divers lusts and pleasures of all kinds" (1 Cor. 6:9-11; Gal. 5:19-21; Eph. 2:1-3; Rom. 1:18-32). He is a "servant of sin" (Jn. 8:34); "unrighteous" (1 Cor. 6:9-11; Ps. 51:5; Eph. 2:1-3); "dead in tresspasses and sins" (Eph. 2:1-9); "alienated from God" by wicked works (Col. 1:20-22); "separated" from God by his sins (Isa. 59:2); "without hope, and without God" in the world (Eph. 2:11-13; 4:13-32; Rom. 3:9-25); "blind to the truth" (2 Cor. 4:4; Eph. 4:18); "lustful" (Eph. 2:3); and "doomed to eternal death and Hell" (Rom. 6:23; Mt. 25:41, 46; Rev. 14:9-11; 19:20; 20:11-15; 21:8; Jude 7; Isa. 66:22-24).

What is Carnality?

The word "carnal" in Romans 8:7 and Hebrews 9:10 is from the Greek word *sarx* meaning "flesh," "the meat of an animal," "the body of any living creature," and "mere human nature," or the earthly nature of man. We have shown in points given above that human nature was originally created perfect and sinless, but since becoming one with Satan and partaking of his spirit and nature, it is now by nature sinful and controlled by evil spirits. Christ had perfect, sinless flesh and human nature by virtue of not being under the control of sin (Rom. 8:3). Thus, *sarx* does not necessarily mean that all flesh is sinful. It is used of the "flesh" of all creatures (1 Cor. 15:39). In Romans 8:7-8 it is the "mind" of the flesh that is sinful because of being controlled by sin (Eph. 2:3). In Hebrews 9:10 it is used of "carnal ordinances," which are not sinful, for they were part of the law which is holy, just, good, and spiritual (Rom. 7:12, 14). They are "carnal ordinances" because they were imposed upon and executed by natural men.

The word "carnal" in Romans 7:14; 15:27; 1 Corinthians 3:1-4; 9:11; 2 Corinthians 10:4; Hebrews 7:16 comes from the Greek word *sarkikos*, which is derived from the root word *sarx*, above. Paul speaks of himself as "sold under sin" and as being "carnal," because of being under the control of the animal appetites, which are controlled by Satan and spirit forces. In Romans 15:27 and again in 1 Corinthians 9:11, the word "carnal" means *the natural things necessary to sustain life*, and the idea could not include sin at all. It means "natural" or "human," without the idea of sin.

Can Christians be Carnal?

Christians can be carnal. In fact, each of us is carnal in some things, for the word simply means "natural" or "human." There are certain natural and human acts that are necessary to all life and conduct. If man had never fallen he would have been perfectly carnal and natural and yet sinless. *All carnality is not sin.* Eating, drinking, sleeping, talking, thinking, walking, sitting, studying, working, and many other activities are perfectly carnal, and yet sinless if done within the bounds of the law. It is only when we use our natural faculties to satisfy our appetites, passions, and desires contrary to the law of God that sin is committed.

Even "sanctified" people in Corinth were called carnal and were accused of walking as men when they had preferences in preachers (1 Cor. 1:2; 3:1-4). It is perfectly natural and understandable to have such preferences. This is why it is carnal and not spiritual. It is not sinful to prefer hearing one preacher above another, unless one makes sin out of it. Such preference becomes sin only when it is carried to the point of division and strife. There is no "sanctified" man who does not have some preferences of this kind, regardless of how many works of grace he may have had. It is like eating food. It is not spiritual to eat food. However, neither is it sin, unless one over–indulges, and then this intemperance is sin. The idea of "carnality," as seen in 2 Corinthians 10:4, is that of human weakness in contrast to divine power. The idea in Hebrews 7:16 is that of natural or human lineage and birth. No sin is involved in this idea, for it is natural and sinless to have offspring according to the law. This Greek word *sarkikos* is translated "fleshly" twice—in the first case, it is used of natural wisdom and knowledge contrasted with grace (2 Cor. 1:12). In the second instance, it is used to describe fleshly lusts (1 Pet. 2:11).

Sinful and Sinless Carnal Acts Distinguished

Thus, when we use the word "carnal" we must keep in mind that sin is not always involved. There can be sinless carnal traits and acts, but the same traits and acts can become sinful when they transgress the law. The following carnal traits show the misuse of human faculties in transgressing the law. These faculties are not sinful in themselves, but become sinful when used to break the law. The unlawful yieldedness of human faculties to commit such things constitutes sin or "transgression of the law" (1 Jn. 3:4). *The spirit and nature of the devil are working constantly to cause men to yield to the following traits of carnality:*

Traits of Sinful Carnality

(1) To feel a secret selfish pride in success or position; in training and appearance; in natural gifts and abilities; and in general standing; to feel an important and independent spirit; stiffness, preciseness, and fault-lessness; to feel an unpleasant sensation in view of another's success or position; to feel over–anxious; and to feel bitterness over the past or over what someone has said or done.

(2) To manifest formality; deadness and dryness in spirituality; indifference to souls and the needs of others; lack of power and spiritual desires; lack of hunger for God; stirrings of anger or impatience; a touchy, sensitive spirit (and worst of all, to call it "nervousness" or "holy indignation"); sharp, heated flings at another; self–will; selfishness; stubbornness; an unreachable, talkative, harsh, sarcastic, unyielding, headstrong, driving, commanding, peevish, fretful, man–fearing, deceitful, proud, malignant, whispering, backbiting, surmising, hateful, boastful, spiteful, disobedient, unmerciful, devilish, and lawless spirit; to manifest a desire to attract attention to self; a desire to dress, act, and be as much like the world as possible; to manifest a love of ease and good things, even at the expense of others more needful; lustful stirrings; unholy actions; undue affections towards those of the opposite sex; uncleanness in thought and desire; unnatural and abusive acts to self and to others; a dishonest, deceitful and evasive spirit; a covering up of real faults and leaving a better impression of self than that which is strictly true; hypocrisy; false humility; exaggeration; straining the truth; unbelief; doubt; fear; lack of confidence in God; worry; constant complaining in pain, poverty, and trials; a desire to quit trying to do right; a dogged determination to deal with others regardless of the outcome to God's cause and the souls of men in eternity.

(3) To have a secret fondness of being noticed; a swelling after freedom in public work or other successes; a desire to make a fair show in the flesh and to do something big in order to call attention to self; darkness in mind and blindness in heart concerning spiritual things; a conscience deadened and hardened that permits

one to commit things which were once given up when first consecrated to God; malice and a "get even" spirit; unforgiveness; a desire for vengeance even to the damnation of one's own soul; unnatural affections; covetousness; maliciousness; emulations; variance; jealousy; envy; evil thoughts; lasciviousness; lustful eyes; blasphemy; foolishness; wrath: strife; seditions; heresies, revellings, drunkenness; a "don't care" attitude toward God and man, toward his responsibilities in life, or when found out in some sin: a shrinking from reproach and duty; reasonings in unbelief about the truth; a disposition to resent and retaliate when crossed; a compromising attitude in order to please men instead of God; and an inferiority complex.

(4)   To be past feeling; unstable in the faith; wandering from church to church; always evading any responsibility for God's work in any one place; unsettled, irresponsible, shallow, and stingy; spineless in spiritual things and in the fight against the flesh, the world, and the devil; satisfied to be a dupe of Satan and take part with those who bite and devour one another and destroy the work of God; vain and light in conversation and manner of life; a joker and a jester, partial to certain persons and classes and in individual dealings; unneighborly, unsacrificing, and unwilling to put self out for anyone else (unless it be to some personal advantage or gain); ashamed of God, Christ, the Bible, the Church and Christianity; fear of spiritual manifestations; thinking always of what might have been if certain things had not happened (instead of realizing that things could be much worse); unthankful and unappreciative; in constant fear of failure to please God, to live righteously, and to walk in the Spirit.

(5) To take an unmerciful attitude in dealing with others who have failed; to take an inferior attitude toward those of wealth or position; and to take a self–righteous, "holier–than–thou" attitude toward those of a weaker or inferior position; to love human praise and supremacy; a need to be coaxed and humored to do things in the church and elsewhere (while at the same time feeling the most capable for the job); to live in abandonment to a lesser degree of blessing than others enjoy, and to come short of God's best in life; to find flaws and criticize when set aside and unnoticed; to find fault with everyone else and in every place; to speak of the faults and failures rather than the virtues of those more appreciated than one's self; to lift self up above others, as being above their faults and failures and as having a spotless record; and to live a life of selfishness and self–gratification.

The effect of such devilish operations are evident to some degree in the lives of all unregenerate men. If those who have experienced salvation do not walk and live in the Spirit, the behaviors and attitudes we have just described will be manifested in them again. These traits are fixed tendencies and habits in fallen man, controlled by the spirit and nature of the devil. Salvation is necessary to break these habits and set man free from such bondage and the operation of sin and Satan in their lives (Rom. 6:1-23; 8:1-13; 2 Cor. 5:17; 1 Jn. 3:8-10; 5:1-5, 18).

Traits of Sinless Carnality

The same faculties used to commit the selfish and unchristian acts mentioned above can also be used in the opposite way. Such manifestations will reveal true

Christian traits and actions that should be a part of every Christian's life. Rather than being sinful, such acts will be righteous and lawful. Study the traits listed above with the idea of practicing the opposite, and one can have a true picture of Christian practices and principles. When we conform our lives to the pattern of Christ and the early Christians, we will be manifesting the true Christian life and will be free from condemnation before God.

The right and lawful acts of creative powers are sinless acts of carnality, because they are natural and normal acts. They are sinless acts because they have not transgressed the law of God. Any human act that is permitted by the law of God is a sinless carnal act, as we have seen in Points 6 and 7, above. One should not feel condemned for anything that is lawful. Sin is only committed when created faculties are used to break God's law. Remember this and the devil will have no grounds for seeking to bring one under self–condemnation or demon–inspired guilt. Satan is the accuser of the brethren and he will constantly seek to bring the believer under condemnation (Rev. 12:10). Unless a definite transgression of the law has been committed there is no sin, so all false demon–inspired accusations can be thrown off when they are suggested to the mind.

All saved men are free to exercise every created faculty within the bounds of the law of God. One can get angry at sin, sickness, and demonic workings—becoming stirred up to the point of action against them—without committing sin. It is not sin to be angry, to be jealous, to love, to hate, or to manifest any natural faculty if one is angry and jealous for a righteous cause. It is not a sin if one loves God and others in a lawful way. It is not a sin if one hates sin and those things God hates. It is all right for one to exercise every faculty and satisfy every appetite, passion, and desire in a lawful way. Let no man ever pray again for God to "de–humanize" or "un–create" him if he is tempted to exercise created faculties. Let him live and walk in the Spirit and control those powers according to the gospel and reject all temptations to use them in breaking the law. Many Christians will be saved a great deal of heartache if they recognize these facts and live accordingly.

Sins that Will Damn the Soul

There are sins that will damn the soul. We find a general list of these in the words of Scripture: idle words (Mt. 12:36-37); evil thoughts, adulteries, fornications, murders, thefts, covetousness, wickedness, deceit, lasciviousness, an evil eye, blasphemies, pride, foolishness, and bearing false witness (Mt. 15:17-20; Mk. 7:19-23); uncleanness, lusts, making God a liar, idolatry, vile affections, a reprobate mind, unrighteousness, maliciousness, envy, debate, deceit, malignity, whisperings, backbitings, hating God; being despiteful, proud, boastful, inventors of evil things, disobedient to parents, without understanding, covenantbreakers, without natural affection, implacable, and unmerciful (Rom. 1:24-32); deceitful tongues, poison lips, cursing mouths, bitter hearts, bloody feet, and ungodly lives (Rom. 3:9-20); being effeminate, sodomites, revilers, and extortioners (1 Cor. 6:9-11); biting and devouring others, witchcraft, hatred, variance, emulations, wrath, strife, seditions, heresies, envyings, drunkenness, revellings, and such like (Gal. 5:15-21); lying, corrupt conversation, resisting the Holy Spirit, bitterness, clamour, evil speaking, and unforgiveness (Eph. 4:25-32); filthiness, foolish talking, jesting, and being a whoremonger (Eph. 5:1-6); inordinate affection, evil concupiscence, anger, and malice (Col. 3:5-9); selfishness, being unthankful, unholy, false accusers, incontinent, fierce, despisers of good people, traitors, heady, high–minded, lovers of pleasure more than lovers of God, having a form of godliness, but denying the power thereof, leading others into sin, faithlessness, and being evil (2 Tim. 3:1-13); brawlers and disobedient, (Titus 3:1-3); having respect of persons (Jas. 2:9-12); living in ungodliness, anarchy, presumption, selfwill, and rebellion (2 Pet. 2:9-22); being lovers of the world and of the things of the world (1 Jn. 2:15-17); filthy dreamers, sowers of discord, hard speakers, murmurers, complainers, and mockers (Jude 8-19); seducers (Rev. 2:20); devil worshippers, sorcerers (Rev. 9:20-21); fearful, unbelieving, abominable, and taking from and adding to the Word of God (Rev. 21:8; 22:18-19).

Biblical Proof That These Sins Will Damn the Soul

There are many statements in the above lists of sins that plainly say that people who commit such things and who die in these sins will be lost. Let the Bible itself prove this by the following passages: "These are the things which defile a man" (Mt. 15:20); "By thy words thou shalt be condemned" (Mt. 12:37); "They which commit such things are worthy of death . . . But we are sure that the judgment of God is according to truth against them which commit such things" (Rom. 1:32; 2:1-2); "For the end of those things is death. For the wages of sin is death" (Rom. 6:16-23); "For if ye live after the flesh, ye shall die" (Rom. 8:12-13); "Know ye not that the unrighteous shall not inherit the kingdom of God?" (1 Cor. 6:9-11); "They which do such things shall not inherit the kingdom of God" (Gal. 5:19-21); "No whoremonger, nor unclean person, nor covetous man, who is an idolator, hath any inheritance in the kingdom of Christ and of God" (Eph. 5:5); "For which things sake the wrath of God cometh upon the children of disobedience" (Col. 3:6); "But the fearful, and unbelieving, and the abominable, and murderers, and whoremongers, and sorcerers, and idolaters, and all liars, shall have their part in the lake of fire" (Rev. 21:8); "The soul that sinneth, it shall die" (Ezek. 18:4); "If any man defile the temple of God, him shall God destroy" (1 Cor. 3:16-17; 6:19-20); "If we deny him, he also will deny us" (2 Tim. 2:12).

Are Bad Habits and Worldly Pleasures Sin?

Worldly pleasures that do not make one spiritual, morally pure, physically clean, or more godly and consecrated to the highest good of all is sinful. Mrs. Wesley gave her children a good rule or test whereby they could know the lawfulness or unlawfulness of a pleasure. It was, "Whatever impairs the tenderness of your conscience, weakens your reason, obscures your sense of God, or dulls your deep desire for spiritual things; whatever increases the authority of your body over your mind and will, that thing to you is sin."

The Bible says, "Love not the world, neither the

things that are in the world. If any man love the world, the love of the Father is not in him. For all that is in the world, *the lust of the flesh*, and *the lust of the eyes*, and *the pride of life*, is not of the Father, but is of the world. And the world passeth away, and the lust thereof: but he that doeth the will of God abideth forever" (1 Jn. 2:15-17); "Know ye not that the friendship of the world is enmity with God? Whosoever therefore will be a friend of the world is the enemy of God" (Jas. 4:4); "And be not conformed to this world: but be ye transformed by the renewing of your mind, that ye may prove what is that good, and acceptable, and perfect, will of God" (Rom. 12:1-2).

Scripture indicates that we are to live our lives very differently from those who don't follow Christ: "If the world hate you, ye know that it hated me before it hated you. If ye were of the world, the world would love his own: but because ye are not of the world, but I have chosen you out of the world, therefore the world hateth you . . . The servant is not greater than his Lord. If they have persecuted me, they will also persecute you; if they have kept my saying, they will keep yours also. But these things will they do unto you for my name's sake' because they know not him that sent me" (Jn. 15:18-21); "The world hath hated them, because they are not of the world, even as I am not of the world" (Jn. 17:14-16).

Can anyone argue scripturally and with a clear conscience that worldly pleasures are of God? Can any claim that they make one spiritual, Christ–like, godly, morally pure, physically better, and the best example for Christians to set before sinners? Can anyone claim that they are definitely of God and helpful in any way to the Christian life? Has anyone ever been saved through any of them? How many hundreds of thousands of sinners stumble daily over church members who indulge in sin? What can such acts be called but lusts of the flesh, lusts of the eyes, and the pride of life?

One only has to look at the lives of godly and consecrated people of God to see the difference between worldly pleasures that draw us toward God and those that draw us away. Why do church members who indulge in worldly pleasures have to always explain and apologize to sinners and real Christians for indulging in such practices? Why do not such church members pray the blessing of God upon such practices when they do them? Why do they feel so condemned for doing such things? Why do many of them seek to hide such practices from real Christians? Why do many of them always want to know whether such practices are sinful or not?

On the other hand, no such questions are ever raised about whether it is wrong to pray, go to church, serve God, and do godly things. Why is it that men who are really saved from their sins and become new creatures have perfect freedom from these habits? Why does God deliver these people from such things if they were godly habits? Why do sinners expect men to be saved from such things when they become Christians? Why do real Christians take up such habits again when they backslide? We all know the answers to these questions, just as we know that such pleasures are sinful and unbecoming to Christians. Therefore, let us all get saved from such habits.

Worldly Pleasures in Churches are Schools of Crime

When children see the world in the churches they are many times turned against Christianity and go into the world when they leave home. I was one of those that rejected Christ for years because of these conditions, and things are infinitely worse in churches today than when I was a boy.

I was brought up in a nice, dignified church where I saw church members participating in activities that were not appropriate for followers of Christ. Many is the time I said, "If that is Christianity, I do not want it." I saw my friends join church, get baptized, and formally accept Christ. I never would join the church. I first wanted to see if religion changed my friends. When I saw them live as they did before, I turned from such hypocrisy and sham and rejected the church for years, until I saw real Christianity in practice. Then I was not long in getting saved from my sins. Sinners are hungry for real Christianity and they will soon accept Christ if men live Christian lives before them.

Movies are Schools of Crime

There are good movies, just as there are good books. Unfortunately, the vast majority of movies coming out of Hollywood are inappropriate for viewing by followers of Christ. That many movies are the schools of crime is a well known fact to those who deal with crime. Many criminals got their start in crime by what they saw on the screen. A Committee of Child Welfare not long ago *(editor's note: Statistical data recorded in this book were accurate as of 1950, the original date of publication)* analyzed 250 American films and found 97 murders, 51 cases of adultery, 19 seductions, 22 abductions, and 45 suicides. The leading characters of these films were: 176 thieves, 35 drunkards, and 25 prostitutes. Roger Babson says, "Such studies as I have made lead directly to the movies as the basic cause of the crime wave today." Turkey, a non–Christian country, passed a bill stating that no children under sixteen shall attend movies. Some of the reasons given were that they distort their brains; shake their nerves; suggest venturous ideas; prematurely convey information about love and love making; inspire violent passions; and lead to crime.

Is this what Christianity stands for? Is this the kind of schools to which we are going to send our children? Do we want to make criminals out of our children? Shall a heathen country be more righteous in its stand against sin than Christians?

It is a known fact that young people practice what they see on the screen. We could give many examples and say many things in support of our claim, but they are well known facts to most everybody, so we will not take up the time and space to relate any more facts. Christians know right from wrong, and it is high time that they either truly get saved and live free from sin or give up the church and show their true colors.

Is Smoking a Sin?

Smoking became known to the civilized world about 1518 A.D. when the tobacco plant was brought to Spain from the Indies. From there it went to France where it was accepted by the Queen Catherine de Medici. After her death the use of tobacco was forbidden by severe laws as being dangerous to the national health. It was first taken to England by Sir Francis Drake in 1586. It was later banished from England and all of Europe for some time. In 1624 Pope Urban the Eighth inflicted corporal punishment and excommunication on all who used it. In 1635 it was again forbidden in France under penalty of imprisonment and public whipping. Periodically from then on various laws for and against it were passed in France. In America, until a couple of generations or so ago, very few used tobacco. Even as late as our present generation most women would not marry men who used it. But today it is glorified as the god of American pleasure and it is becoming difficult to find men or women who do not use it in some form or another. In 1949, 400 billion cigarettes were used in America alone, besides tobacco in other forms. It is popular for preachers and church members to go about using it, and men who raise a voice against it are labeled old–fashioned, out of date, and religious cranks.

Be that as it may, we must stick by true Christian principles. It cannot glorify God, as Christians are commanded to do in their bodies and spirits (1 Cor. 6:19-20). It defiles their bodies, and God promises to destroy those who defile His temple, the human bodies (1 Cor. 3:16-17). It is a money–wasting habit. Men must satisfy their lust even at the expense of bread, proper clothes, and shelter for the family. It is an infringement on the rights of others who should not be forced to constantly breathe smoke wherever they go (Gal. 5:14). It is a wrong example to set before sinners (Mt. 5:16). It is a filthy habit and

Christians are commanded to cleanse themselves "of all filthiness of the flesh and spirit, perfecting holiness in the fear of God" (2 Cor. 7:1). It is a filthy and unclean habit and is one of the works of the flesh under the word "uncleanness" (Gal. 5:19-21). It is a bad habit and holds one in bondage to sin (Rom. 6:12-23).

Tobacco Poisons the Body and Causes Disease

Tobacco is a poison and is listed along with all other poisons. In fact, it contains nicotine, prussic acid, ammonia, carbolic acid, acrolein, carbon monoxide, formis aldehyde, methylamine, marsha gas, furfural, and parvolin. Webster lists it as a narcotic. Nicotine alone is so deadly that one–fifteenth of a grain will kill an adult and half this much will kill a dog. There is enough in one cigar to kill a man if he chewed and swallowed it. Of course many have become used to much of the effects of these poisons. These poisons cause cancer, heart trouble, shattered nerves, blood poisoning, stomach disorders, skin diseases, and in general poisons the entire system. To say the least, it is unbecoming to Christians and brings reproach on the cause of Christ.

We spend four billion dollars a year on tobacco (in 1950)—twice as much as we pay public school teachers. Two out of every three men and two out of every five women smoke, and 800,000 non–smokers are being added to the ranks yearly.

When a person smokes, most of the nicotine escapes into the air. About one–third gets into the mouth, where little is absorbed. The effect of smoking a cigar is equal

to that of five cigarettes. A pipe gives a trifle more nicotine than does a cigar. In pure form nicotine is a violent
poison. One drop on a rabbit skin throws the rabbit into
instant shock. The nicotine content of two cigarettes,
if injected into the bloodstream, would kill a smoker
swiftly. If you smoke one pack a day, you inhale 400
milligrams of nicotine a week, which in a single injec-
tion would kill as quick as a bullet.

In factories which make nicotine insecticides, cases of
poisoning occur now and then. One worker sat on a stool
which held a little spilled nicotine. In less than two minutes he fell to the floor blue in the face, apparently dead.
Rushed to the hospital, he was revived as one does from
slight nicotine poisoning. When he returned to the shop
and put on the nicotine soaked trousers he fell headlong
on the ground, and had to be revived a second time.
Out of the 400 billion cigarettes smoked a year there
are nearly 23 million gallons of nicotine. Administered
with precision, this is enough to kill a thousand times
the population of the United States.

Why doesn't smoking kill more people? Partly
because the remarkable human body can gradually
build up a tolerance for larger and larger doses of poison; partly because, in smoke, it is not accumulated in
sufficient quantities.

Do cigarettes irritate the throat? No doctor claims that
smoking soothes the throat. The argument hinges upon
how much they irritate the throat, If you smoke a pack
a day, you take in 840 cubic centimeters of tobacco tar
in a year. That means you have drenched your throat
and lungs with 27 fluid ounces of tobacco tar during
the year. In 100 smokers who averaged 28 cigarettes a

day, Dr. Frederick B. Flinn of New York found 73 with congestion of the throat, 66 with coughs, and seven with irritation of the tongue. Doctors familiar with the field comment on how many times smokers change brands to find a less irritating cigarette. It is also a known fact that cigarettes affect the stomach and digestion. It interferes with the appetite, causes gastritis, heartburn, stomach ulcers, non-development of the bodies of growing people, hinders athletic performances, lowers muscular power, causes fatigue, speeds the pulse as much as 28 beats a minute, affects the heart and blood stream, causes irregularity of the heart, raises the blood pressure, markedly and quickly, constricts the blood vessels and often closes completely the smaller ones in the hands and feet.

Smoking causes Buerger's disease, which is a loss of circulation of the hands and feet, and sometimes causes gangrene which makes amputation necessary. Out of 2,400 cases of this disease that were tested, everyone was a smoker. A group of 100 cases were studied for ten years and in all of them the disease was arrested when smoking stopped. Three cases out of the 100 had to have parts of the body amputated, and these were the only three that would not stop smoking, according to Dr. Irving Wright. Heart disease is more prevalent among smokers than non-smokers. It is also a known fact that cancer of the lungs, throat, lips, and other parts of the body are caused by smoking.

Why do not physicians warn their patients more helpfully about smoking? Because doctors are human, too, and many of them smoke; because many of them hesitate to believe the worst about the friendly cigarette;

and, as one physician noted sadly, "Because forbidding tobacco makes a doctor unpopular."

The writer of the article in the *Reader's Digest* from which is taken most of the above facts says, "When I began a research of this article, I was smoking 40 cigarettes a day. As I got into the subject, I found that number dropping. As I finished the article, I am smoking ten a day. I'd like to smoke more, but my investigation of the subject has convinced me that smoking is dangerous and, worse—stupid."

This comes from a smoker and not from a preacher whom many smokers consider as unqualified to speak on the subject. Those who want to please God and truly serve Him can be delivered from the desire to smoke by confessing his sins to God and getting the new birth that we will consider in the next two chapters.

Chapter Six

HOW TO GET RID OF SIN

There is a sure cure for sexual lusts, unclean living, worldly pleasures, and all sins and bad habits in Jesus Christ. Men can be saved and delivered from the power and dominion of these things in an instant—by a full surrender of their lives to God and by getting the genuine new birth, which we shall discuss below. The power of such habits can be broken if one will take the divine method of deliverance from sin, sickness, and bad habits. Such sins will be hated by those who have really been saved and born again.

When We are Saved from Sin and Bad Habits

At the time of the new birth, or when one asks for forgiveness of sins, he should renounce all sin and make up his mind he will not hold on to even one bad habit. If he will cut loose from all old friends and places of sin and make a complete surrender of his life to God he will be saved from all sin.

If new converts will go to God in prayer and ask for deliverance in the name of Jesus Christ it will be granted. If temptation lingers, rebuke the unclean demons of nicotine, alcohol, or whatever the lust may be. Rebuke them in the name of Jesus Christ, commanding them to loose their hold on the body and they will go. James and Peter said, "Resist the devil and he will flee from you" (Jas. 4:7; 1 Pet. 5:8-9). Be definite and strong in resistance and no power of sin or habit will remain in you.

Why Some Men are Not Saved from All Sin

One must realize that these habits are sinful and unlike Christ and then they will not be hard to resist in prayer for deliverance. But as long as one still wants to hold on to some bad habit and still maintain contrary to his conscience and the truth that it is not sinful, he will never get deliverance. Such has to be rejected because of obedience to the truth and because of wanting to be a true clean Christian, then God will deliver at once. If the habit persists after this, then go to a church where the preacher and members believe in deliverance from such habits and have them lay hands on you and rebuke the demon power which binds men by such habits.

Others are not delivered from all sin because they join churches that believe one must sin every day and that no man can live without sin. They are not taught what deliverance from sin really is, so they do not get saved from all sin. They do not feel any condemnation by indulging in bad habits because they see many church members doing the same things. Consequently, they hold on to their old habits and claim to be saved. There is no excuse for their ignorance of what a true Christian life is or of what God demands men to give up when they become Christians. Such men are not using the intelligence God gave to them. Just because many church members (and even preachers) commit sin, this is no reason why the real true Christian should live contrary to the will of God.

The fact is, many thousands of church members in America—even many preachers—do not know any more about salvation from sin as a personal experience than a heathen living in the jungles of Africa who has never heard of Christ. Many of them are honest enough to acknowledge that they do not know what it is to be born again and to be saved from all sin. Many of them are deceived in believing that if they join a certain church and live a good life that they will be saved. Many actually believe that because they have been baptized or have conformed to certain creeds that they are saved. But the truth of the Bible is that no man is saved until he has been born again by the Spirit of God and has quit all of his sins. This we shall prove below by many plain Scriptures.

Salvation Necessary

It is time that men wake up to what the Bible teaches and forget what some churches hold as the standard of Christianity. If there is a way of knowing one is saved, then he should be honest enough to acknowledge that he is not saved until he has met the requirements of the Bible. One can meet the requirements of church membership of many denominations and still be lost. We are warned in Scripture that if the blind lead the blind both shall fall into the ditch (Mt. 15:14). All the excuses under the sun for not doing what God plainly says will not get that person by the judgment bar of God. God has made Himself clear concerning entrance into the kingdom of God, and He knows full well that all men have intelligence enough to understand His written requirements and He will hold them to His Word in the end. It matters not how much you love a preacher, a church, or some church member, or how much you have confidence that they must be right, it will pay each person to check, and double check, what he is being taught and what he is depending upon to save his soul in the end. One can know that he is right, not by what any man says, but by the Bible.

The Real Reason for Sin in the Church

The reason many thousands are in doubt as to whether they are really saved and born again is because they have never experienced biblical salvation. It is impossible for any man to really experience salvation from sin and not know it. If anyone is in doubt whether he has ever been saved or not, it is clear that he is not saved. He should frankly acknowledge that he has not been truly saved from sin, or he would know it. As soon as he becomes honest enough to acknowledge it and asks God to save him and make him to know it, the more quickly he will become satisfied. Men who have a definite experience of salvation are never in doubt about it.

The Story of Old George Nye

Some 23 years ago we pitched a tent in Sand Springs, Oklahoma, for a revival meeting. Nearly every night during the testimony meetings when opportunity was given for Christians to tell what God had done for them, an old man by the name of George Nye would get up with tears running down his cheeks and make comment on his favorite hymn. He described it as: "There ain't a friend like the lowly Jesus, no, not one! no, not one!" He would then tell the following story, as well as I can remember it. "About eight years ago Jesus Christ saved me from a life of sin. I used to tramp the streets of Tulsa (about eight miles from Sand Springs) and steal milk bottles, rakes, hoes, lawn mowers or anything that I could get my hands on in order to get a little more dope to keep me alive. I was a dope fiend and one of the lowest kind of sinners. I had such a record of arrests in Tulsa until they would seldom bother me any more. I was always getting into jail and out again. I had to have dope or I could not live. The craving for dope was so strong until it would force me to do anything to get more of it. I never will forget my last friend. He was an old black dog that followed me through the streets of Tulsa. I would live out of the garbage pails and sleep in the streets at nights. One day I lay in the gutter at the corner of First and Main streets. I was under the influence of dope and whiskey until I hardly knew what I was doing. I got so low that my last friend left me. My old black dog looked at me and wagged his tail and walked off. I never saw him again. After some time I got up and staggered down the street. I heard the Salvation Army singing, 'There ain't a friend like the lowly Jesus.' I went with them to the hall and there I staggered up to the altar and gave my heart to Jesus Christ. He saved me from all my sins. I had no more desire for tobacco, whisky, dope, or any other sin. I have been serving the Lord for about eight years and He is so good to me. I am always happy and am working every day. I now have a nice place to stay and plenty of food to eat and clothes to wear. He is such a wonderful Saviour. He can save anyone that will come to him."

We soon learned that "old George" (as he was called) was a trusted servant of the multi–millionaire oil man, Charlie Page, who was also a great philanthropist of Tulsa and Sand Springs, Oklahoma. George was the private mail carrier for this man, traveling between Tulsa and Sand Springs. Mr. Page had a widow's colony and an orphan's home that he supported, besides many other projects to help the poor. One day Mr. Page invited us to eat Sunday dinner at the orphanage. At the table across from this millionaire sat old George. Mr. Page said to us, "That man is a marvel of the grace of God. He has been my trusted mail carrier for eight years. I have trusted him with thousands of dollars. I have never lost one penny in all these years. I would trust him with all that I have."

Anyone could ask old George if he knew whether he was saved or not and he would soon tell you. He would tell you in no uncertain terms that if you were saved you would know it. What a pity that thousands of church members today are uncertain of their relationship to God. Multitudes think they are saved when they are not. It will pay everyone to do whatever necessary in order to be assured of old–fashioned salvation. Let no man think that he cannot know. Neither let any man trust that he is all right if he does not know that he is saved and born again. If one will confess his sins and mean business with God, he can be assured beyond all doubt that he is saved.

Soul Salvation All-Important

The question of eternal life and personal welfare is all-important. At least, it is important enough for us to make sure that we are right with God. We should determine this solely by the Bible and not by what a certain preacher, church, or religion has said on the subject. Many are so foolish. They will trust their eternal soul to a man or to the teaching of some religion, but they would not blindly follow this policy with their business. If some preacher or religion told him how to run his business and he had all his wealth invested in the business, he would be a fool to blindly follow such teaching without proper investigation and proof that his wealth is secure if such instructions were followed. There would be ways of finding out whether such advice is right or wrong, and every businessman would see to it that it was right before following such counsel. He should be just as business-like when it comes to his eternal soul. He should spend days and nights, if need be, with the Bible to see if he is being taught truth and whether or not he has conformed to what the Bible plainly teaches. Then he could know beyond all doubt as to his true standing before God and the judgment.

Chapter Seven

THE DOCTRINE OF THE NEW BIRTH

The following studies on the new birth will make it clear that a man must be saved from all sin and how this can be brought about in his life so that he will know it:

The Absolute Necessity of the New Birth

Jesus taught that a man "must be born again" and "Except a man be born again, he cannot see the kingdom of God . . . Except a man be born of water and of the Spirit, he cannot enter into the kingdom of God . . . Except ye be converted, and become as little children, ye shall not enter into the kingdom of heaven . . . Except ye repent, ye shall all likewise perish" (Jn. 3:1-8; Mt. 18:3; Lk. 13:1-5).

We repeat again, it is all–important that we pay personal attention to our eternal welfare and not trust the best of men. If we permit men to mislead us in eternal matters and we are lost, it will be too late to see after our welfare; so let us do it now. Don't take the attitude that you cannot be deceived and that your church is the only right one and cannot mislead you. This may be true, but it would be wise for you to make sure of it by going to the Bible for yourself and seeing with your own eyes and knowing from your own heart that you are right with God and that you have had a real new birth and that you are living right with God every day. Don't let any religion make you think you are all right just because you have conformed to its teachings. You may still be lost. Make sure about it.

There is no use fooling yourself. That will not get you anywhere except to eternal Hell. You are either born again or you are not. You are either really saved, or you are being deceived into thinking that you are, or you know that you are lost. If you are not getting answers to your prayers, it is either that you are not saved, or you are doubting God. If your obstacle is doubt, then you should quit doubting God. If it is not doubt, then it will pay you to examine yourself, and see if you are really right with God. He is obligated to answer you if you are His child. If you have once been saved, it may be that you have become cold in your experience and need to reconsecrate your life to God. You know your own life and true relationship to God; so get the fact settled that you are a genuinely saved person and in present contact with God, and then you will be in the right position to get what God has promised.

Thus, it is clearly stated that the new birth is a necessity if one wants to be reconciled to God. No person can be saved without it. No person can get to Heaven without it. It is the one "must" of the Christian faith, so it is critically important that we learn everything we can about the new birth—and get it—in order to be eternally saved.

What the New Birth is Not

The new birth is *not* confirmation, church membership, water baptism, signing a card stating that you accept Christ, taking the sacrament, shaking hands with the preacher, standing up to accept Jesus as a saviour, observing religious duties, an intellectual reception of Christianity, orthodoxy of faith, confessing Jesus as the Son of God, joining some church that claims to be the true church, going to church, saying prayers, reading the Bible, memorizing creeds, being moral, being cultured or refined, doing good deeds or doing your best, being as good as the next fellow, or any of the other things that some men are trusting in to save them outside of old–fashioned religion and the experience of the new birth as stated in Scripture.

Neither is the new birth brought about by these things. Nicodemus, whom Jesus addressed concerning the new birth, had most of these qualifications, but Jesus said to him, "Ye must be born again." The thief on the cross and many others whom Jesus forgave while on Earth were saved without these things. They simply did the one necessary thing—became "converted" and "born again"—by accepting Jesus Christ as their personal Saviour and by repenting and turning to God with their whole heart as a little child, as proven in Matthew 9:1-7; Luke 7:48-50; 18:9-14; 23:43; and John 8:1-10.

Every man who is born again will automatically have the external evidences of a good life by virtue of the new birth, but there are millions, it is sad to say, that are trusting these things to save them, and they really believe that these things are the evidences of a right relationship with God. Millions will die and be lost without the new birth because they have been misled concerning the experience of being born again. There is no excuse for men being deceived if they will read their own Bibles instead of listening to some religious teacher. One can have all the forms of religion and still be lost in eternity without God and without hope.

Culture, refinement, and outward correctness of life in the church or out of it will not take the place of the new birth. The trouble is in the heart (Mk. 7:18-23), and merely to reform the outward life will not save the soul.

An artist could put a coating of wax and the most beautiful colors on the outside of a rotten apple, but it would still be rotten at heart. One bite into it would be a bite into decay. The fact is that out of Christ every man is rotten in the heart, and mere culture, refinement, outward respectability, morality, and outward correctness of life are simply artificial and the practice of hypocrites, who, like whited sepulchres, "make clean the outside; but within are full of extortion and excess . . . dead men's bones, and all uncleanness" (Mt. 23:25-28; Rom. 3:9-23).

What the New Birth Is

The new birth is a new creation from above through a direct operation of the Word of God and the Holy Ghost upon the life, changing a person completely and making him a new creature in Christ. It is the same as the new creature experience of 2 Corinthians 5:17; the new creation work of Ephesians 4:24; the salvation experience of Romans 1:16; 10:9-10; 2 Thessalonians 2:13; the baptism in the body of Christ of 1 Corinthians 12:13; Galatians 3:27-29; the experience of being made free from the law of sin and death of Romans 8:1-4;

the adoption into the family of God of Romans 8:14-16; the turning from Satan to God of Acts 26:18; the washing from all sin of 1 Corinthians 6:9-11; 1 John 1:7-9; Revelation 1:5; the remission of sins of Acts 2:38; the reconciliation to God of Colossians 1:20-23; 2 Corinthians 5:17-21; and the begetting of one as a child of God of 1 Peter 1:2-4, 18-23; and James 1:18.

How the New Birth is Received

The new birth is brought about by four acts on the part of man. When any man does these four things he can be assured that he is born again of the Spirit of God and that he has been accepted into the family of God. *The four acts are:*

(1)   Recognize that you are a sinner and lost, without God and without hope (Rom. 3:23; Eph. 1:11-13; 1 Jn. 1:9). One time in South Dakota a church member came down to an altar of prayer. I asked her what she came for and she said that she wanted to get the good feeling that some of the Christians say they have. I asked her if she was a sinner and she replied that she had been born a Christian. Her parents were members of such and such a church and she was brought up in the church and had never sinned in her life. I told her that she might as well go back to her seat since real salvation and knowledge of sins forgiven is only for sinners. She repeated that she wanted the wonderful experiences that she knew others had. I told her that she could not have them because such blessings were only for sinners. I knew she was deceived into thinking that because she was brought up in a church that she was born a Christian and was not

a sinner. I then asked her if she had ever gossiped. She replied, "I guess everybody has done that." I asked her if she had ever lied. She replied, "No." I said, "You mean to tell me that you have *never* told even a white lie, or you have *never* misrepresented anyone or anything or tried to deny any wrong doing in all of your life?" "Oh," she said, "I guess we have all tried to get out of acknowledging wrong things that we have done." I asked her several other questions about personal sins and she acknowledged that she had done all those things at times in her life. I told her that this was enough to convince her that she was a sinner and needed salvation, and if she did not believe she was a sinner because of her doing wrong many times in her life that the Bible says that she was a sinner, for "all have sinned and come short of the glory of God" (Rom. 3:23). If a person will not acknowledge that he is a sinner, he cannot be saved.

(2) Admit that Jesus Christ died on the cross to save you from sin by His own precious blood (1 Pet. 1:18-23; 2:24; 1 Jn. 1:7-9; Eph. 1:7).

(3) Come to God repenting of your sins and turning away from all sin, pleading the merits of the blood of Christ in the name of Jesus Christ, and you shall be born again; that is, the Holy Spirit will then definitely make you a new creature, cleansing you from all sin by the authority of the Word of God and by the blood of Christ that was shed to atone for your sins (2 Cor. 5:17; Eph. 4:24; Col. 1:20-22).

(4) You must believe from the heart when you confess with the mouth that God does forgive you of your sins and that He does cleanse you from all unrighteousness (Rom. 10:9-10; 1 Jn. 1:7-9; 5:1-4).

When one does these four things, yet he still does not know that he is saved, something is wrong with him and not with God. There is something in his life that he has failed to confess or make right with God or with his fellow men. If one is willing to forgive all others of their trespasses against him, as required in Mark 11:22-26, and if one is willing to give up all sin and bad habits and turn to God with their whole heart to obey God and the Bible, he will definitely be changed in life by the power of God. But if one holds on to something or is not willing to forgive others, he cannot be saved.

Some years ago in Pennsylvania, while preaching what men must do to be saved from sin, a woman yelled out in the audience with a loud voice, "I can't!" Without knowing what she referred to I answered, "You can!" She continued to say, "I can't!" Three or four times we answered each other this way. Finally I said, "Sister, what is it you cannot do?" She said, "I can never forgive him." I learned afterward that her husband had left her for another woman and she had determined in her heart that she would never forgive him. I said, "You have to forgive him in your heart before God will forgive you." She said, "I will go to Hell before I forgive him." Whether she ever forgave him or not I do not know, but if she does not she will be lost, according to Jesus (Mk. 11:22-26).

One time in South Dakota two girls came down to the altar of prayer for salvation. One was forgiven in a few minutes and rejoiced in her salvation. The other did not get satisfied that night or the next night, or the third night, until I found out what was wrong. On the third night I said to her, "Young lady, you might as well tell me what is wrong. There is no need for you to come for prayer every night if you do not mean business. Your friend got gloriously converted in a few minutes the first night when you both came together to find Christ. She has found Him and you have not." She replied, "I don't know what is wrong." I said, "You do not need to tell me that. You *do* know what is wrong or you would not be having such a struggle. God is no respecter of persons. If He saved your friend He will save you, if you are willing to give up what He asks of you. Is there anyone you are not willing to forgive?" She said, "No." I replied, "Is there anything you are not willing to give up?" She replied, "Yes, there is a young man that loves to take me to the dances. I love to dance." I then showed her that the dance, and even a young man that would leave her if she stopped going to dances, were not worth losing her soul over. She then accepted Christ and gave up the dance and was soundly converted. And so it is, any person can be saved—and know it—if he or she will mean business with God and surrender all sin to live holy according to the gospel.

This method of getting men saved is not the modern way that great evangelists use, who require only the raising of a hand, a hand shake, or the formal and mental acceptance of Christ by acknowledging that He is the Son of God, but this method will produce sound and saved converts in every case. It may be that a few really get saved by a formal acceptance of Jesus or by saying that they take Jesus as a Saviour, but in the majority of cases this method is too shallow and produces only church members without old fashioned salvation that will make them new creatures. This is why such converts so often continue in their same sin and bad habits.

They did not get saved from their sins to begin with. They had no power of deliverance from their sins and habits, and consequently soon realize that they did not get what they needed. Preachers are responsible for leading them this far and no further. They are responsible for not teaching them what salvation is all about and what is expected of them when they turn to God.

It is the habit of the modern preacher to emphasize that all one has to do to be saved is to merely say that he accepts Christ. Men can do this daily without a change of heart. This is the easy way; the way of least effort on the part of man, and this is why he gets so little, or nothing, in so many cases. If all men were required to really repent and pray until they knew that God had forgiven them and until they received the evidences of the new birth (as we'll see in Chapter Eight), then we would not have so many sinning Christians; that is, people who are sinners and who claim that they are Christians. As we see in the following Scripture, when men find biblical salvation, they will stick with it and forsake sin:

> For godly sorrow worketh repentance
> to salvation not to be repented of: but
> the sorrow of the world worketh death.
> *2 Corinthians 7:10 KJV*

Many thousands never repent of sins, as the Bible demands. They merely say to the preacher that they accept Jesus. Some do not do anything but answer the preacher's question of: "Do you accept Jesus as your Saviour?" They say "yes" and that is all there is to getting right with God. There is no repentance or godly sorrow for sin, no giving up sin, and no real consecration to God. There is more to salvation than this. Men must repent and quit the sin business. They must seek God until they are new creatures.

What the Water of the New Birth Means

The Word of God is the "water" referred to in John 3: 5, as proven in Ephesians 5:26; Jn. 6:63; 15:3; 17:17; 1 Peter 1:23; and James 1:18. When one believes the Word of God . . . that he is a sinner, that Christ died to save him from all sin, that if he confesses his sins to God and turns from sin with a whole heart and believes the gospel . . . he is conforming to the Word, then the Holy Spirit will transform him by faith in the power of the Word of God and the blood of Christ and give him the evidences of salvation as listed below. One must get a Bible experience and live as God demands or be lost. He must begin reading the Bible and praying to God. He must begin to walk and live in the Spirit and conform to the Word of God as he receives the light (1 Jn. 1:7; Jn. 8:31-32).

Chapter Eight

EVIDENCES OF THE NEW BIRTH

There are certain evidences of the new birth that are plainly stated in Scripture that will prove to the individual and to others that he has been born again.

Biblical Evidences of the New Birth

(1) *You will be changed down in the depths of your being and be made a new creature:* "Therefore if any man be in Christ, he is a new creature: old things are passed away; behold all things are become new. And all things are of God, who hath reconciled us to himself by Jesus Christ" (2 Cor. 5:17-18). If you have never been changed like this, then it is certain that you have never been born again.

(2) *You will have the witness of the Spirit in your life that you are a child of God:* "For as many as are led by the Spirit of God, they are the sons of God. For ye have not received the spirit of bondage again to fear; but ye have received the Spirit of adoption, whereby we cry, Abba Father. The Spirit himself beareth witness with our spirit, that we are the children of God" (Rom:8:14-16).

(3) *You will have freedom from condemnation and from the law of sin and death and you will live and walk in the Spirit:* "There is therefore now no condemnation

to them which are in Christ Jesus, who walk not after the flesh, but after the Spirit. For the law of the Spirit of life in Christ Jesus hath made me free from the law of sin and death . . . That the righteousness of the law might be fulfilled in us, who walk not after the flesh, but after the Spirit. For they that are after the flesh do mind the things of the flesh; but they that are after the Spirit, the things of the Spirit . . . And if Christ be in you the body is dead because of sin; but the Spirit is life because of righteousness" (Rom. 8:1-13; Gal. 5:16-26).

(4) *You will be cleansed from all sin:* "He shall save his people *from* their sins" (Mt. 1:21); "The blood of Jesus Christ cleanseth us *from* all sin . . . If we confess our sins, he is faithful and just to forgive us our sins, and to cleanse us *from* all unrighteousness" (1 Jn. 1:7-9).

(5) *You will be free from sin:* "Ye shall know the truth, and *the truth shall make you free* . . . If the son therefore shall make you free, *ye shall be free indeed*" (Jn. 8:31-36); "Shall we continue in sin, that grace may abound? God forbid. How shall we that are dead to sin, live any longer therein? . . . Our old man was crucified with him that the body of sin might be destroyed, that *henceforth we should not serve sin.* For he that is dead *is freed from sin* . . . Reckon yourselves to be *dead indeed unto sin . . . sin shall not have dominion over you* . . . Know ye not, that to whom ye yield yourselves servants to obey, his servants ye are to whom ye obey; whether of sin unto death, or of obedience unto righteousness? . . . ye were the servants of sin . . . being made *free from sin,* ye became the servants of righteousness . . . even so now yield your members servants to righteousness unto holiness. For when ye were the servants of sin, *ye*

were free from righteousness . . . but now being made free from sin, and become servants to God, ye have your fruit unto holiness, and *the end* everlasting life" (Rom. 6:1-23); "The law of the Spirit of life in Christ Jesus *hath made me free from the law of sin and death*" (Rom. 8:1-4); "Everyone that *doeth righteousness* is born of him . . . he that doeth righteousness is righteous *even as he is righteous* . . . He that committeth sin *is of the devil* . . . whosoever is born of God *doth not commit sin* . . . whosoever is born of God *overcometh the world* . . . whosoever is born of God *sinneth not*; but he keepeth himself, and that wicked one *toucheth him not*" (1 Jn. 2:29; 3:7-10; 5:1-4, 18).

(6)   *You will be delivered from the power and dominion of sin:* "For sin shall not have dominion over you: for ye are not under the law, but under grace" (Rom. 6:14. See also passages from the last point, above).

(7)   *You will receive power to become a son of God:* "But as many as received him, to them gave he power to become the sons of God, even to them that believe on his name" (Jn. 1:12; 2 Tim. 1:7; 1 Jn. 3:1-3).

(8)   *You will receive a definite crucifixion of the flesh with the affections and lusts:* "They that are Christ's have crucified the flesh with the affections and lusts" (Gal. 5:24; Eph. 4:22-24; 2 Cor. 5:17).

(9)   *Your sins will be blotted out:* "Repent ye therefore, and be converted, that your sins may be blotted out, when the times of refreshing shall come from the presence of the Lord" (Acts 3:19).

(10) *You will be washed, sanctified, and justified:* "And such were some of you: but ye are washed, but

ye are sanctified, but ye are justified in the name of the Lord Jesus, and by the Spirit of our God" (1 Cor. 6:11).

(11) *You will have salvation:* "That if thou shalt confess with thy mouth the Lord Jesus, and shalt believe in thine heart that God hath raised him from the dead, thou shalt be saved. For with the heart man believeth unto righteousness; and with the mouth confession is made unto salvation" (Rom. 10:9-10); "But we are bound to give thanks always to God for you, brethren, beloved of the Lord, because God hath from the beginning chosen you to salvation through sanctification of the spirit and belief of the truth" (2 Th. 2:13).

(12) *You will be created in righteousness and true holiness:* "And that ye put on the new man, which after God is created in righteousness and true holiness" (Eph. 4:24).

(13) *You will depart from iniquity:* "No man that warreth entangleth himself with the affairs of this life; that he may please him who hath chosen him to be a soldier . . . Nevertheless the foundation of God standeth sure, having this seal, The Lord knoweth them that are his. And, Let every one that nameth the name of Christ depart from iniquity" (2 Tim. 2:4, 19).

(14) *You will have God the Father, God the Son, and God the Holy Spirit dwelling in you:* "Jesus answered and said unto him, If a man love me, he will keep my words: and my Father will love him, and we will come unto him, and make our abode with him" (Jn. 14:23); "But ye are not in the flesh, but in the Spirit, if so be that the Spirit of God dwell in you. Now if any man have not the Spirit of Christ, he is none of his" (Rom. 8:9).

(15) *You will be free from the power of Satan:* "To open their eyes, and to turn them from darkness to light, and from the power of Satan unto God, that they may receive forgiveness of sins, and inheritance among them which are sanctified by faith that is in me" (Acts 26:18).

Do Born Again People Sin Daily?

I am fully aware that many teach that no man can live free from sin, that we sin every day, and that there is no one that does not sin every day he lives. One can see that this teaching is entirely out of harmony with the Bible by reading the above Scriptures. If these men sin every day, then they are sinners every day and there is no time that they are not sinners. If they are sinners all the time, then there is no time they are not under the penalty of the broken law, and they will be sent to Hell as sinners to pay the death penalty. They are not Christians or saved from sin any one day they live if they sin every day they live. Christ means nothing to them if they are sinners and if they cannot be saved from sin.

It is time that men wake up and stop listening to such teaching and begin to read the Bible and obey it for themselves. Naturally, no man that does not believe in salvation from sin can ever get saved from sin. If Christ came to save us from our sins and He cannot do it, then He has failed in His mission. If the New Testament teaches freedom from sin, then it is either the truth or a lie. If it is a lie, then we might as well throw the whole Bible away and have nothing to do with religion. Christianity, in that case, is a mere sham and a false religion, teaching something that is not true. If salvation through Christ is true, however, then these modern teachers of religion are false and no man can safely believe them. It is not right even to listen to them deny the truths of the Bible. It is a sin to support them in such a program. If Christianity is a sham, it is a sin to support it and its leaders.

Do not let men deceive you into thinking that there is no such thing as a clean, holy, and victorious life in Christ, secure from sin, the flesh, the world, and the devil. If you are not saved from these things you are not saved from Hell, according to the Scriptures under Point 10, Chapter Five. There may not be such a life of freedom from sin as far as these teachers are concerned and as far as they know. Either they do not know the Bible and they do not have biblical experiences, or they are plain rebels against truth and refuse to get such blessings. In either case, you should not listen to them concerning such an important thing as your eternal welfare. Why not listen to the Scripture instead? It will not deceive you. It will always tell you the truth, as you can see from Scriptures in Point 1, above.

The other day a young man called to question my Bible doctrine of a Christian being free from sin. I named adultery, fornication, and all the sins listed under Point 10, Chapter Five, and asked him in connection with each one of them if he were guilty of these sins. He said he was not guilty of them. I asked if he was committing these sins daily and he said he was not. I asked him if he thought he could live free from these sins daily, and he said that he could. He said that he was a Christian and that the only thing he knew he was doing that could be wrong was smoking. I asked him if he thought he could get rid of that and live free from it every day. He answered that he could. I then asked him if he thought he would be living free from sin if he were free from all these sins, and he answered in the affirmative and agreed that such a life was possible.

People who think they cannot live free from sin are really mistaken as to what sin is. If they consider lack of knowledge, temptations, and common mistakes that do not break the law of God as sin, then they are right to believe that no man lives free from sin. But if they think one cannot live free from the soul–damning sins mentioned above, then they are wrong, for such must be true of anyone who will be saved. Those who argue that no one can live without sin are simply using every excuse under the sun to continue in sin. They want to make people believe that they are Christians, and yet they want to indulge in some sin or bad habit that will condemn them in the end. Men can live free from sin if they get saved from sin and permit Christ to live in their lives by the power of the Holy Spirit. If men live in sin daily then there is not a day in which they are not under the condemnation of a broken law and they will be sent to Hell to pay the death penalty for sin.

Is the Body Sinful and the Soul and Spirit Holy?

The theory that the body is always sinful and the flesh sins every day, but the soul and spirit are perfectly sinless and holy, is one of the most foolish, ignorant, and unscriptural theories the devil and his agents are seeking to impose upon intelligent Bible–loving people. There can be no Scripture produced that says any such thing.

This is purely a doctrine of demons to deceive men and cause their souls to be lost in eternal Hell. *The following Scriptures prove that the body must be holy and sinless as much as the soul:*

"Knowing this, that our old man is crucified with him, *that the body of sin might be destroyed*, that henceforth we should not serve sin. For he that is dead [that is, dead to sin as in Rom. 6:2] is freed from sin" (Rom. 6:6-7); "If Christ be in you, *the body is dead because of sin*; but the Spirit [Holy Spirit] is life because of righteous- ness . . . Therefore, brethren, we are debtors, *not to the flesh, to live after the flesh. For if ye live after the flesh, ye shall die*: but if ye through the Spirit do mortify *the deeds of the body*, ye shall live" (Rom. 8:1-4, 10, 12- 13); "I beseech you therefore, brethren, by the mercies of God, that ye present *your bodies a living sacrifice, holy, acceptable unto God*, which is your reasonable service. *And be not conformed to this world: but be ye transformed* by the renewing of your mind, that ye might prove what is that good, and acceptable, and per- fect, will of God" (Rom. 12:1-2); "*The body is not for fornication, but for the Lord*; and the Lord for *the body* . . . Know ye not that *your bodies* are the members of Christ . . . Every sin that a man doeth *is without the body* . . . *Your body* is the temple of the Holy Ghost, which is in you, which ye have of God, and ye are not your own? . . . Therefore glorify God in *your body*, and in *your spirit*, which are God's" (1 Cor. 6:13, 15, 19-20); "Know ye not that ye [*your bodies*] are the temple of God, and that the Spirit of God dwell in you? If any man defile *the temple of God*, him shall God destroy; for *the temple of God is holy*, which temple ye are" (1 Cor. 3:16-17); "But I keep under *my body*, and bring it into subjection:

lest that by any means, when I have preached to others, I myself should be a castaway" (1 Cor. 9:27); "That the life also of Jesus might be manifest *in our body*" (2 Cor. 4:10); "Christ shall be magnified *in my body*, whether with the circumcision made without hands, *in putting off the body of sins of the flesh* . . . having forgiven you all trespasses" (Col. 2:11-13); "that she may be holy *both in body and in spirit*" (1 Cor. 7:34).

Are All Christians Holy?

One of the great scarecrows of modern religion is the word "holiness." People of various churches are more afraid of this word or the word "holy" than they are of the very devil himself. In fact, many would rather have fellowship with the devil than anyone who believes in holiness. There are many holiness denominations that are looked upon as the offscouring of all things and as the refuse of all that is evil. Why not be fair and honest a few minutes and consider with us what God says on the subject. Now, don't misunderstand, we are not advocating some of the peculiarities of certain groups that call themselves "holiness." We are not suggesting that you have to be branded as such before you can be saved and be holy, according to the Bible. We merely want to point out that there is no reasonable excuse for anyone to be afraid of the words "holy" and "holiness." No man needs to think that holiness is going to jump on him and take him to Hell without his consent. One can only become holy in Christ and by full obedience to the gospel. It will not fall upon anyone. It is not some devil that seeks entrance into the lives of men. Devils are in the business of keeping men from becoming holy, hence, the great scare that they have caused among honest people. They do not want you to live any kind of life that even looks like it is holy, so just calm yourself and don't be afraid you will get something wrong while we consider what God says.

Believe it or not, everyone who is a real Christian is holy and, therefore, is a holiness person. This is true whether he is a Baptist, Methodist, or Presbyterian. This is proven by the Scriptures in points given above. If men today get the salvation of the New Testament they will be holy. The words "holy" and "holiness" are used in the following passages, which prove that all children of God are holy people:

"That we . . . might serve him without fear, *in holiness and righteousness* before him, all the days of our life" (Lk. 1:74-75); "Even so now yield your members servants *to righteousness unto holiness* . . . ye have your fruit *unto holiness*, and the end everlasting life" (Rom. 6:16-23); "For if the first fruit *be holy*, the lump is *also holy*: and if the root *be holy, so are the branches*" (Rom. 11:16); "Present *your bodies* a living sacrifice, *holy*, acceptable unto God" (Rom. 12:1); "Ye are the temple of God . . . the temple of God *is holy, which temple ye are*" (1 Cor. 3:16-17; 6:19-20); "That she may *be holy* both in body and in spirit" (1 Cor. 7:34); "Cleanse ourselves from all filthiness of the flesh and spirit, *perfecting holiness* in the fear of God" (2 Cor. 7:1); "He hath chosen us in him before the foundation of the world, that we should *be holy and without blame* before him in love" (Eph. 1:4); "And that ye put on the new man, which after God is created *in righteousness and true holiness*" (Eph. 4:24): "That it [the church] should *be holy and without blemish*" (Eph. 5:25-27); "To present you *holy and unblameable and unreproveable* in his sight" (Col. 1:20-23; 3:12); "For God hath not called us unto uncleanness, but *unto holiness*" (1 Th. 4:3-7); "I charge you by the Lord that this epistle be read unto all *the holy brethren*" (1 Th. 5:27); "I will therefore that men pray everywhere, lifting up *holy hands*, without wrath and doubting" (1 Tim. 2:8); "She shall be saved in childbearing [from death in child birth], if they continue in faith and charity *and holiness* with sobriety" (1 Tim. 2:15); "Who hath saved us, and called us with an *holy calling*" (2 Tim. 1:9); "A bishop must be blameless . . . sober, just, *holy*, temperate" (Titus 1:8); "That they be in behaviour *as becometh holiness* . . . Teaching us, that denying ungodliness and worldly lusts, *we should live soberly, righteously, and godly, in this present world*" (Titus 2:3, 11-14); "Wherefore, *holy brethren*, partakers of the heavenly calling . . . Follow peace with all men, *and holiness, without which no man shall see the Lord*: Looking diligently lest any man fail of the grace of God" (Heb. 3:1; 12:10, 14); "But as he which hath called you *is holy, so be ye holy in all manner of conversation* [manner of life] . . . Ye also, as lively stones, are built up a spiritual house, *an holy priesthood*" (1 Pet. 1: 15-16; 2:5, 9; 3:5; 2 Pet. 3:11).

In the light of such clear Scriptures, can anyone with a clear conscience claim to believe the Bible and still deny that Christians are (and must be) holy to be saved in the end? These passages speak for themselves—they demand holiness from every believer. If men are not holy, they are not saved; if they are saved, they are holy. In fact, every person who is born again *is* holy according to the passages cited above and 1 John 2:29; 3:5-10;

5:1-4, 18; 2 Corinthians 5:17; Galatians 5:24; etc. No man will have any part in the first resurrection without holiness of life: "Blessed *and holy* is he that hath part in the first resurrection: on such the second death hath no power, but they shall be priests of God and of Christ, and shall reign a thousand years" (Rev. 20:4-6; 22:11).

Some will argue that no man can be holy and live free from sin, but it is certainly clear that no man who does not live this way will ever see God in peace. If men cannot live this way, then there cannot be any such thing as Christians—either now or in eternity. Men do not have to belong to any particular group labeled "holiness," but it is certain that without being holy in God they are lost. Therefore, let us all become holy in Christ and be more tolerant toward other holy people.

The "new birth" means more than the mere profession that Jesus is the Son of God. Neither does it mean that one is saved because of church membership, water baptism, church attendance, partaking of the Lord's Supper every Sunday, or a lot of other substitutes that some men are trusting in to save their souls. One must experience salvation the "Bible way" or be lost.

We have given you the truth about the new birth, salvation, and how to live a sanctified life in Christ to the end. The responsibility of conforming to truth is yours. You will be saved or lost as you accept the message of God and obey the gospel. Give your heart to God and do not be satisfied with anything short of becoming a new creature in Christ, and then you can experience eternal life.

Chapter Nine

THE DOCTRINE OF FAITH

It is God's Will for All Men to Have Faith

It is the will of God for all of His people to have unwavering, unshakeable, and absolute faith in Him. It could not be anything but His will for all men to have faith in Him. Could it be possible that God would rather have unbelief in Him than to have faith? Would God rather have men doubt Him (calling Him a liar in everything He says) than for them to have utmost confidence in Him? Could it be the highest will of God for men to question everything that He says rather than to accept it as truth? Shall men pray to know whether it is the will of God for them to have faith? Shall they constantly pray, "If it be thy will, O God, please show me whether it is thy will for me to have faith in you and your Word"?

In answer to these questions, I hear you say, "Certainly not, no one should pray such a prayer! We should have faith in God and in what He says without praying to know whether it is His will or not." This is true, and undoubtedly this is what anyone would answer if they were asked the same question. Yet some will still argue that it is difficult to have faith in God, that they cannot have faith enough to get answers to prayer, that they cannot know whether it is the will of God to do what

He has promised, that they cannot get their prayers answered and they don't know what is wrong.

Only One Cause for Failure in Prayer

There is only one cause for failure in prayer. Jesus taught that it was "Because of your unbelief." Some argue that this cannot be the trouble in their case, but the fact remains that this is the sole reason, providing one is a qualified child of God. Suppose we search the Scriptures for some other reason and see if it can be found . . . suppose we investigate what God says and give Him the benefit of any doubt. If we would answer ourselves with the Bible we would find a number of Scriptures that plainly prove this.

Scriptural Proof Unbelief is the Cause of Failure

When the disciples proved powerless to cast out the devils from the lunatic boy they came to Jesus and said, "Why could not we cast him out?" Jesus said to them, "Because of your unbelief: for verily I say unto you, If ye have faith as a grain of mustard seed, ye shall say unto this mountain, Remove hence to yonder place; and it shall remove; and nothing shall be impossible unto you" (Mt. 17:19-20); "Jesus answered and said unto them, Verily I say unto you, If ye have faith, and doubt not, ye shall not only do this which is done to the fig tree, but also if ye shall say unto this mountain, Be thou removed, and be thou cast into the sea; it shall be done. And all things whatsoever ye shall ask in prayer, believing, ye shall receive" (Mt. 21:21-22); "Jesus said unto him, If thou canst believe, all things are possible to him that believeth" (Mk. 9:23); "And Jesus answering saith unto them, Have faith in God. For verily I say unto you that whosoever shall say unto this mountain, Be thou removed, and be thou cast into the sea; and shall not doubt in his heart, but shall believe that those things which he saith shall come to pass; he shall have whatsoever he saith. Therefore I say unto you, What things soever ye desire, when ye pray, believe that ye receive them and ye shall have them" (Mk. 11:22-24); "But without faith it is impossible to please him: for he that cometh to God must believe that he is, and that he is a rewarder of them that diligently seek him" (Heb. 11:6); "If any of you lack wisdom, let him ask of God, that giveth to all men liberally, and upbraideth not; and it shall be given him. But let him ask in faith, nothing wavering. For he that wavereth is like a wave of the sea driven with the wind and tossed. For let not that man think that he shall receive any thing of the Lord. A double minded man is unstable in all his ways" (Jas. 1:4-8).

Do Not Make God a Liar

Are we going to believe these passages or are we going to argue with God and contend with the Almighty concerning His Word? If God says that we can have what we want if we have faith, then if we do not get what we want it is certainly *because of unbelief.* When we say that God will give all men the answer to their prayers if they pray in faith, we want to make it clear that we refer to children of God only. God has not promised to hear every prayer that a sinner prays, except for the prayer of repentance when asking forgiveness for sin. Sinners cannot have unwavering faith in God for those things promised to Christians. Faith is the gift of God and one must be qualified as a child of God to have faith to claim the full benefits of the promises of God. As long as we argue that God will not hear every prayer of every truly saved child of God who prays in faith according to the promises of God, we make God a liar. Since some Christians are not finding many of their prayers answered—because of unbelief and doubt, we suggest that they try another method—taking God at His Word with unwavering faith, not because they merit anything, but because of the clear written Word of God.

The Definition of Faith

The words "faith," "trust," and "believe" simply mean "to confide in, so as to be secure without fear;" "to flee for refuge to" or "to take shelter in;" "to put faith in;" "to stay or rest on;" "to rely on;" "to believe or to take one at his word;" "to rely upon the promise of another;" and "to put absolute trust in a person without any questioning or doubts as to His faithfulness."

In the King James Version of the Bible, *faith* is defined as, "The substance of things hoped for, the evidence of things not seen" (Heb. 11:1). Various translations of the Bible express this verse in a number of ways. Some of the variations are as follows: "Now faith is a well–grounded assurance of that for which we hope, and a conviction of the reality of things which we do not see" (Weymouth); "Now faith means we are confident of what we hope for, convinced of what we do not see" (Moffatt); "Now faith is the title–deed of things hoped for; the putting to proof of things not seen" (Centenary Translation); "Now faith is an assumption of what is being expected, a conviction concerning matters which are not being observed" (Concordant Version); "Now faith is the persuasion of the things that are in hope, as if they were in act; and it is the manifestness of the things not seen" (The Syriac); "Now faith is assurance of things hoped for, a conviction of things not seen" (Revised Version).

The Nature of Faith

Paul, in Romans 4:17, teaches that true faith is an attribute of God, "who quickeneth the dead, and *calleth those things which be not as though they were.*" Faith is a union of assurance and conviction; the counting or reckoning a thing done as though it were already done. Faith does not have to see before it believes. It laughs at impossibilities and all circumstances that may be contrary to it and counts the thing done that it asks from God. Faith is not swayed to believe God only when things seem possible. It is not moved to waver or question in the least when things seem to go contrary to what has been asked. It doggedly plugs right along counting the impossible as possible; counting as done the things that are not seen; and counting the things that are not as though they were.

What Faith is Not

Faith is not *feeling* that prayer is answered. The average person who seeks to exercise faith depends upon what he can see, hear or feel. Testimonies concerning faith are usually expressed in connection with feelings and emotions, or the various senses. "Sense faith" is based upon physical evidence or upon the emotions and feelings of the soul. All who take this road as the basis of faith will sooner or later be deceived. Faith should be based upon the Word of God regardless of any sense–knowledge, or feeling–evidences. People are constantly looking to feelings as to whether prayer has been heard or not. If they happen to feel good, or if something happens that encourages them, they think that it is easy to believe, but if reverses come and feelings take wings, these same people are plunged into the depths of despair. They are quick to accuse God of being unfaithful and untrue to His Word. If they do not go this far, they are quick to imagine that it was not God's will to grant the answer. They become satisfied to live without those thing that God has plainly promised.

Faith Related to the Human Senses

Faith has no relationship with feelings or the evidence of the senses. During those times when we feel that we have abundant faith, we may have the least in the world. Likewise, when we think we have the least, we may have more faith than at any other time in our lives. Many people are surprised to receive answers to prayer, thinking that when they prayed they had no faith. We should not believe we are healed because the pain is gone, nor should we believe that we are saved just because we feel forgiven. We should not think that our prayers are answered because things are working out that way. Instead, we should always maintain that our prayers are answered because the Word of God says they are.

The Word of God should have first place in our lives, instead of our senses. Basing our faith on what we have done, how well we live, or what experiences we've had will lead to failure in prayer. God does not answer upon these grounds. He answers solely upon the grounds of grace and personal faith in Him and His Word.

Faith Must Be in the Right Objects

Not only must we have personal faith, but faith must be in the right objects. Our faith must be "in God" (Mk. 11:22-24); "in Christ and His atonement" (Acts 3:16; Rom. 3:25); "in the Holy Spirit" (1 Cor. 12:1-11; Gal. 5:22); and "in the Word of God" (Rom. 1:16). We must choose to believe God regardless of anything that might happen to hinder prayer. Rather than talking about faith, or the need for it, we should be involved in the actual exercise of it. Simple faith in the Word, regardless of feelings and circumstances, is never possible for the man who lives only in the realm of his senses, for he believes only what he can see, feel, hear, or understand to be possible. This was the kind of faith Thomas had when he declared that he would not believe until he had seen. It was the kind that Martha had when she could see nothing but the natural fact that Lazarus had been dead four days and "by this time he stinketh." This is the kind of faith taught and encouraged by modern religious leaders, but it is not the kind required by the New Testament.

The Right Kind of Faith is Necessary

Active, living faith is necessary in order to obtain

answers to our prayers. We must learn to use this kind of faith in God. We must learn to fight the fight of faith and lay hold of God and His Word. We must learn that we are surrounded by an unbelieving world and that we live in an atmosphere of doubt. Demons, fallen angels, and men have lived for centuries in unbelief and wickedness, creating currents of doubt and mistrust that are very subtle and deceiving to those who desire to have faith. The fall of man has left deep wounds of doubt that must be healed. We must learn that we have to wrestle with powers of darkness and currents of mistrust and unbelief, which make it a struggle to exercise active living faith for things that are not seen. We must not only learn *how* to do this, but we must *do it* in order to get results.

Weak Faith
(Rom. 4:19; 14:1–15:4; 1 Cor. 8)

Weak faith constantly limits the benefits we receive and the appropriation of the privileges granted us as followers of Christ. Weak faith is due to wrong teachings and personal scruples concerning many non–essentials. Many are the church members who spend their time arguing and condemning each other over things so insignificant that they are not even mentioned in Scripture. These arguments consist of what one may or may not eat, drink, wear, or do and still be a Christian. In Romans 14 it is clear that the kingdom of God does not consist in meat, drink, and personal details of life that are not specifically forbidden in Scripture, but that it is "righteousness, and peace, and joy in the Holy Ghost."

If the devil cannot get men to commit sins that are

forbidden in Scripture, he will urge honest–hearted people to condemn personal liberties that are not strictly forbidden by God. The law of Scripture concerning anything that is not definitely forbidden by God in Scripture is: "He that doubteth is damned if he eat, because be eateth not in faith: for *whatsoever is not of faith is sin*" (Rom. 14:23).

The Christian law of love for others is: "Let us therefore follow after the things which make for peace, and things wherewith one may edify another. For meat destroy not the work of God. All things are pure; but it is evil for that man who eateth with offence. It is good neither to eat flesh, nor to drink wine, nor any thing whereby thy brother stumbleth, or is offended, or is made weak. Hast thou faith? Have it to thyself before God. Happy is the man that condemneth not himself in the things which he alloweth. We then that are strong ought to bear the infirmities of the weak, and not to please ourselves. Let every one of us please his neighbor for his good to edification" (Rom. 14:19-22; 15:1-2).

Strong Faith
(Rom. 4:20)

Strong faith is the kind that refuses to be defeated. It refuses to take "no" for an answer. It laughs at circumstances, outward appearance, and what is seen or felt, and it doggedly holds to the fact that what has been asked of God is granted. Abraham had this kind of faith: "Who against hope believed in hope, that he should be the father of many nations, according to that which was spoken, So shall thy seed be. And being not *weak in faith*, he considered not his own body now dead, when he was about an hundred years old, neither yet the deadness of Sarah's womb [who was about ninety years old]: He staggered not at the promise of God though unbelief; but was *strong in faith*, giving glory to God; and *being fully persuaded* that, what he had promised, he was able also to perform. And it was counted to him for righteousness" (Rom. 4:18-22).

This is the kind of faith all men should have—and can have—if they will only persuade themselves that God is true to His Word. Most men claim to have faith in God to this extent, and no one wants to boldly state that God is a liar and that He will not do as He has said, but when it comes to exercising unwavering faith, few will maintain a faith strong enough to thank God for the answer even before it is realized. Fewer still will simply refuse to question or waver when it seems that things are going contrary to what has been asked of God. This is exactly why many do not receive definite answers from God. There is no person who will exercise faith as strong as that of Abraham, who will go very long without an answer from God. Such a thing, that God would refuse one who came to Him in such unwavering faith, is literally impossible and unheard of (Jas. 1:4-8; Heb. 11:6). All men are definitely assured of getting from God those things which He has promised if they will "walk in the steps of that faith of our father Abraham" (Rom. 4:12, 23-25).

Unfeigned Faith
(1 Tim. 1:5; 2 Tim. 1:5)

Unfeigned faith is the kind that knows no hypocrisy, sham, or counterfeit. It is faith that does not brag or put on an outward show. It is simply genuine and real and sincere in its every aspect. It proceeds out of a pure heart and from a good conscience, as stated in these Scriptures. It is not hereditary, although in 2 Timothy 1:5 Paul speaks of it as being in three successive generations. It is the kind that all honest, pure, and sincere men have. It is the unselfish, holy, and godly kind that naturally increases in the life of every true child of God, as he grows in grace and knowledge (2 Pet. 1:4-9; 3:18).

Temporary Faith
(Lk. 8:13)

Temporary faith is the kind of faith that believes for a while and springs up like a mushroom, but because of shallowness, or lack of root, it fails in time of temptation and test. People through the ages have been of this type. They receive the Word of God with great joy, and it seems that they will outstrip everyone in their zeal and faith, but after a few days or weeks they are not heard of again except, perhaps, following another revival meeting where their emotions again become stirred to make another start in faith, only to fall again. They never fully "come clean" with God or make the full surrender of their lives except for the moment. They do not prepare the soil so that the seed can take deep root and produce fruit.

Some teach that this cannot happen, but it does—in spite of the so-called impossibility of falling away from the faith and being renewed in repentance again. Some teach that one cannot fall from the faith, but Jesus certainly said that some would "receive the word with joy; and these have no root, *which for a while believe,* and in time of temptation *fall away*" (Mt. 13:20-21; Lk. 8:13). Paul speaks of these as those who "concerning faith have made shipwreck" (1 Tim. 1:19); as having "cast off their first faith" by going "aside after Satan" (1 Tim. 5:12-15); and as having "erred concerning the faith" (1 Tim. 6:21). Many Scriptures say that men can depart from, and fall from the faith (Acts 14:22; 1 Tim. 2:15; 4:1; 5:8-15; 6:10, 21; 2 Tim. 2:18; Heb. 3:6, 12-14; 6:11-12; 10:22-38). We are repeatedly told to continue in the faith (Acts 14:22; Col. 1:23; 2:6-7). It is clear that we can disbelieve anything that we choose to lose faith in, especially in things that are not seen.

Mental or Historical Faith
(1 Jn. 5:10-13)

Mental faith is faith in the history, or the record of God, concerning the past and concerning His own work. We can believe mentally the record of God and still not be saved. It is simply believing with the mind the record of anything of the past. No consecration to God is necessary to believe history. Mental faith may believe every part of the Bible, past, present, and future—and all the truth of the blessings of God—but if it does not act upon the Word of God, it falls short of true heart faith. Faith without works is dead, being alone. It is passive or mere mental assent to truth. Thousands of sinners have mental faith in God and the Bible, but they keep neglecting the definite action of obeying truth.

True faith is not only mental assent to truth as a fact. Most people have such assent. They will believe that God is able, that He has promised to do certain things, and that

He would if true faith were exercised, but there is little effort put forth to cooperate with God or to obtain what He has promised. It is merely a mental assent to truth without active faith in it. It is the kind of faith that will turn to every source of help but God, and His Word. It is just like believing that food is good without ever eating to get the benefits from it. Mental assent, or passive faith, is one of the most dangerous enemies of true faith in God. It claims all the faith in the world and is satisfied easily with either anything or with nothing from God. If it does not get what it wants, it does not care. It would accept something from God if He would come personally and lay the answer in the lap, but apart from this there is little or no effort put forth to act in faith concerning anything God has promised. Mental faith may go as far as to maintain belief in every truth and in every part of God's program, and it may even claim to be contending for certain benefits, but as long as it remains in the mind, it will not dare to act upon the promises of God.

Active Faith
(Jas. 2:14-26; Heb. 10:19-39)

Active faith acts upon the Word of God as it is made clear. James put it this way: "shew me thy faith without thy works, and I will shew thee my faith by my works." Everyone must have this faith to receive anything from God. As long as faith is purely mental and passive, no action will be taken to obey the truth. We must move beyond the stage of hearing only and into the act of doing what God says before we see any results. Active, living faith moves to obey every truth of God and to appropriate what God has promised. It acts as if the things that are not seen are a reality. It is quick to provide works to prove that it is sincere and obedient.

Think of having a real, active, living faith of your own! Imagine the thrill of having your own prayers answered! As I write I have on my desk a large stack of letters marked "Testimony." These letters, which have been received in recent months, tell how God has answered prayer. People hear the radio programs and are inspired to take God at His Word. And as they act, their prayers are answered.

One lady says that she had been sick for ten long years and had not done any of her housework. She heard me say on the air that if you will believe God and refuse to be sick and defeated, you can have whatever you want. She said, "I acted upon the Word and got out of bed and God met my faith. I have been doing my work ever since." Another one is so thrilled that her prayers have been answered three times from laying her hands on the radio and praying with us. Many more are deeply stirred to a new life and deeper consecrations because they are learning to act upon the Word.

Multitudes of people have never had an answer to prayer, and they are missing the greatest blessings of life by such neglect. Most people depend upon others to get answers for them. They pray, so they think, but they want someone else to do the believing. In reality, they are not praying. They are merely saying words and going through a form of prayer. True New Testament prayer is always heard of God and the answer is always sure. God has planned that all men should have this kind of faith and results. "These signs shall follow them that believe," and "all things are possible to him that believeth" (Mk. 9:23; 11:22-24; 16:15-20; Jn. 14:12-15; 15:7-16).

Faith can be developed into a mighty living force that will know no defeat. You can know that you are master of all demonic powers and every circumstance through Jesus Christ. You no longer need to be a slave to fear, timidity, weakness, failure, sickness, poverty, helplessness and despair. You can be a conqueror in the very things wherein you have suffered defeat. "If you abide in me, and my words abide in you, ye shall ask what ye will, and it shall be done unto you" (Jn. 15:7, 16).

You must awake to the consciousness of the new life you have in Christ. As a branch, you have His life, His health, His power, His love, and His nature flowing through you. You are the fruit–bearing part of Christ in the Earth. You are in Him and He is in you. You have His words abiding in you, giving you faith for whatsoever you ask. You have as much right in Him to be asking and receiving from God as He had. You have a right to expect the same answers from God that He received. You represent God here as He did, so do not be satisfied to go without the benefits that He died to give to you.

You are commanded to be a doer of the Word, and this means *ask* and *receive*. You are not to be merely a bearer. You are not deceiving yourself when you act upon the Word. It will be confirmed, for it is truth (2 Cor. 1:20). It must be a living, active faith, not a mere mental passive something that all sinners can have. You are in Christ, and as God's child and heir you have the authority to act on the Word. You are a fruit–bearer, a producer for God, so get busy and produce for Him according to His Word (Jn. 15:1-16).

Wavering Faith
(Jas. 1:5-8)

Wavering faith is faith doubting God and refusing to believe. To believe and to have faith is to act on the Word. It means taking what is already yours. To believe on Jesus means to take Him for all that the Bible declares Him to be. It means that you take salvation from sin, healing for the body, answers to your prayers, and all that He died to bring to you. Believing is an act of the will. When you really believe, you have acted. You have taken the necessary step to get what you want from God. Faith is action in counting those things that be not as though they were (Rom. 4:17; Mk. 11:22-24). Doubting is refusing to act on the Word. Unbelief is either refusing to act according to the knowledge that you have, or it is a manifestation of ignorance of the Word of God. If you do not know, you cannot act because you do not understand. If you do not understand, you are afraid to act because you do not know how to act. The cure for unbelief is a thorough knowledge of the Word and consecration to obey it to the letter, regardless of how impossible it may seem to you at the moment.

A wavering faith is called double–mindedness, a constant change of the mind as to what is wanted or whether the thing asked for is wanted or not. It is the attitude of yes–no, yes–no, and yes–no, until God Himself cannot tell whether it is yes or no. One minute it is decided that a thing is wanted, and it may be wanted with some real desperation, but the next minute it is not so important and it does not matter much whether it is received or not. People who have wavering faith do not really make up their minds that they are going to see the fight of faith through to an answer. They would accept the answer if it would come without any effort on their part, but are not willing to take the necessary steps to obtain an answer.

Unwavering Faith
(Heb. 10:23; 11:6)

Unwavering faith is faith taking God at His Word without question. God commands us to "ask in faith, nothing wavering. For he that wavereth is like a wave of the sea driven with the wind and tossed. For let not that man think that he shall receive any thing of the Lord. A double minded man is unstable in all his ways" (Jas. 1:5-8). We are told to "Hold fast the profession of our faith without wavering; (for he is faithful that promised)" (Heb. 10:23). Again, "But without faith it is impossible to please him: for he that cometh to God must believe that he is, and that he is a rewarder of them that diligently seek him" (Heb. 11:6).

This is faith—refusing to doubt, wonder, question, or reason about any detail of what one has asked from God. Faith has absolute confidence that what was asked is according to the Word of God, and therefore it knows that prayer is answered. It rests upon the promises as the basis of the answer, instead of upon feelings and physical senses. It refuses to act contrary to what it has asked or to question any delay in receiving an answer. It counts the thing done regardless of all outward evidences to the contrary. It laughs at impossibilities and goes on in utmost confidence that what God has promised, He is able to perform. True faith gives thanks for the answer from the moment it asks and looks forward in child–like expectation of getting it.

Human Faith
(Mk. 11:22-24)

Human faith is simply the exercise of our human faculties in the confidence and conviction that we can believe God, and that God is true to all that He has promised. All of us are capable of having faith in ourselves and faith in anyone else that makes a statement of promise to us. Faith is an attribute of man's created being. It was natural for man to believe God before the fall. There was no such thing as doubt or unbelieving reasoning on the part of man before this time. It was the devil that injected doubt and unbelief into man's moral and spiritual makeup. Since man's fall, and because of the almost total depravity of his being, it becomes one of the greatest struggles of his redemptive career to have that same simple, unwavering faith that was natural before the fall. It was doubt and unbelief that caused the fall, and it is of the greatest importance to get rid of all such in redemption.

Divine Faith
(Heb. 11:3; 12:2; Gal. 2:20; 5:21; 1 Cor. 13:14)

Faith is not only a natural attribute of man, it is an attribute of God. It is God's absolute confidence and conviction in His own Being and Word. The first passage listed above teaches that the ages were planned by faith through the Word of God and that things were brought into existence that never existed before. God had faith in Himself when He planned the worlds. He believed that He could do what He commanded, and He "calleth those things that be not as though they were" (Rom. 4:17). The third passage listed above speaks of "the faith of the Son of God," thus proving that He also has faith as does the Father. In fact, He is the author and finisher of faith (Heb. 12:1-2). The last passage mentioned above speaks of "faith" abiding along with hope and love, which means that these three qualities are eternal as attributes of God.

Chapter Ten

HOW TO OBTAIN AN ANSWER TO EVERY PRAYER

There are several things we must do before we can receive answers to our prayers. In fact, there are some things we must do to be heard of God at all. Let's look at how simple it is to pray and receive answers to prayer.

It is God's Will to Answer Every Prayer

The first thing to do is to believe that God wants to answer every prayer; that is, believe it is God's will to answer all who pray to Him in faith in the name of Jesus Christ according to His promises. It is God's highest will for every man to receive the answer to every prayer that he prays, provided he prays correctly. How do we know that it is God's will to grant every prayer if it is prayed right? We know this from the plain written Word of God. God has promised to answer every prayer of His children who pray in harmony with His Word. *To prove this, note the following passages in the Bible:*

Scriptural Proof that it is God's Will

"Ask, and it shall be given you; seek, and ye shall find; knock, and it shall be opened unto you: . . . For every one that asketh receiveth; and he that seeketh findeth; and to him that knocketh it shall be opened . . . Or what man is there of you, whom if his son ask bread, will he give him a stone? . . . Or if he ask a fish, will he give him a serpent? . . . If ye then, being evil, know how to give good gifts unto your children, how much more shall your Father which is in heaven give good things to them that ask him?" (Mt. 7:7-11)

"And Jesus said unto them, Because of your unbelief: for verily I say unto you, If ye have faith as a grain of mustard seed, ye shall say unto this mountain, Remove hence to yonder place; and it shall remove: and nothing shall be impossible unto you" (Mt. 17:20)

"Jesus answered and said unto them, Verily I say unto you, If ye have faith, and doubt not, ye shall not only do this which is done to the fig tree, but also if ye shall say unto this mountain. Be thou removed, and be thou cast into the sea; it shall be done . . . And all things, whatsoever ye shall ask in prayer, believing, ye shall receive" (Mt. 21:21-22)

"Jesus said unto him, If thou canst believe all things are possible to him that believeth" (Mk. 9:23)

"And Jesus answering saith unto them, Have faith in God . . . For verily I say unto you, That whosoever shall say unto this mountain, Be thou removed, and be thou cast into the sea; and shall not doubt in his heart, but shall believe that those things which he saith shall come to pass; he shall have whatsoever he saith . . . Therefore I say unto you, What things soever ye desire when ye pray, believe that ye receive them, and ye shall have them" (Mk. 11:22-24)

"Verily, verily I say unto you, He that believeth on me, the works that I do shall he do also; and greater works than these shall he do; because I go unto my Father . . . And whatsoever ye shall ask in my name, that will I do, that the Father may be glorified in the Son . . . If ye shall ask any thing in my name, I will do it . . . If ye love me, keep my commandments" (Jn. 14:12-15)

"If ye abide in me, and my words abide in you, ye shall ask what ye will, and it shall be done unto you . . . Ye have not chosen me, but I have chosen you, and ordained you, that ye should go and bring forth fruit, and that your fruit should remain: that whatsoever ye shall ask of the Father in my name, he may give it you" (Jn. 15:7, 16)

"And in that day ye shall ask me nothing. Verily, verily, I say unto you, Whatsoever ye shall ask the Father in my name, he will give it you . . . Hitherto have ye asked nothing in my name: ask, and ye shall receive, that your joy may be full" (Jn. 16:23-26)

"But without faith it is impossible to please him: for he that cometh to God must believe that he is, and that he is a rewarder of them that diligently seek him" (Heb. 11:6)

"If any of you lack wisdom, let him ask of God, that giveth to all men liberally, and upbraideth not; and it shall be given him . . . But let him ask in faith nothing wavering. For he that wavereth is like a wave of the sea driven with the wind and tossed . . . For let not that man think that he shall receive any thing of the Lord . . . A double minded man is unstable in all his ways" (Jas. 1:5-8)

"For if our heart condemn us, God is greater than our heart, and knoweth all things. Beloved, if our heart condemn us not, then have we confidence toward God. And whatsoever we ask, we receive of him, because we keep his commandments, and do those things that are pleasing in his sight" (1 Jn. 3:20-22)

"And this is the confidence that we have in him, that, if we ask any thing according to his will, he heareth us: And if we know that he hear us, whatsoever we ask, we know that we have the petitions that we desired of him" (1 Jn. 5:14-15)

What could be clearer than these passages to prove that it is the will of God to grant the answer to every prayer? Could it be possible that God said things in these passages that He did not mean? Shall we further question the will of God in this matter, or shall we believe the simple promises which express the will of God concerning prayer?

Think of it! Anything and everything that one wants he can have through prayer if he will but ask in faith, nothing wavering! This is the right way to pray. This is the requirement of God and the only thing He requires of His children. Of course, we must be finished with sin before we can be called a child of God and before we can pray in the right way. God has not promised to answer the prayers of those who rebel against Him, although these too will receive answers to some prayers. They can have forgiveness (and this should be received before one can expect answers to all prayers). The heathen pray, but are never heard and answered of God like He will answer the prayers of Christians. The reason is that they do not recognize Jesus Christ, through whom men must come in order to receive from God. No man can approach God except through Jesus Christ (Jn. 14:6; 16:23-26).

What Prayer Really Is

A true knowledge of what prayer really means is important and necessary. Prayer is the offering up of our desires for lawful and needful things and things we want that are promised by God, with humble confidence that we will obtain them through Jesus Christ for God's glory and for our good. It is the pleading of our cause in God's court. Prayer is seeking help from God in matters that are beyond our power. It is the personal appeal to a present God based upon His will and Word and our lawful desires. It is cooperation with God's willingness to manifest His goodness to all those who have faith in Him and depend upon Him for help. Prayer is simply *asking* and *receiving* from God, and that is the theme of this chapter.

The Importance and Power of Prayer

There can be no greater thing accomplished in life than to learn to pray aright and to realize the importance and power of prayer. The importance of prayer can be easily understood when we come to know that anything and everything we possibly can want in this life can be received through prayer. This enables us to realize the tremendous power of prayer. The energy of prayer is even greater than atomic energy. Prayer will move Heaven and Earth and bring everything to us that we command that is covered by the promises of God. It matters not what the need is (or even what the want is), prayer will bring it to pass.

If you are sinful and bound by vile habits and passions, prayer will break every fetter in a moment of time. This has been proven by the conversions of the vilest and lowest sinners that have ever lived, as we have already seen. If you want healing for the body, prayer will make you perfectly whole, as we shall see in Chapters Eleven through Thirteen. If you want success in business, prosperity, and freedom from failure in this lifetime, prayer will bring it about. This we shall see in Chapter Fifteen. "All things are possible to him that believeth," and this takes in anything that needs to be done in human experience.

The Art of Prayer Must Be Mastered

Prayer is a real art that must be learned before we can receive anything that we want from God. It is simply the act of a child receiving things from his father. This illustrates the true relationship between God and the one who prays (Mt. 7:7-11). One must learn to draw nigh to God and rely wholly upon Him for needed grace for body, soul, and spirit (Jas. 4:7-10). One must become skilled in faith and prayer and cease all doubting, as we have seen in previous chapters; then prayer will become a simple transaction between God the Father and His child.

In learning to pray, one must practice prayer until he becomes perfect. It is like learning to do any other thing. One can learn all about prayer, but without frequent practice the art of prayer will never be perfected. Concentrate upon prayer whenever time permits. Even learn to pray while at work. This can be done with great profit. One can work better or do anything much better if he will learn to pray at all times. Prayer is being in perfect union and harmony with God and naturally those in perfect harmony can do things better. One will succeed in life to the extent in which he harmonizes with God and His creation.

Make prayers as simple and definite as possible. Turn all your problems over to Him. Depend upon Him to help you and He will. Do not be afraid to take even the smallest problem to Him, for He cares and is pleased when we have simple childlike faith in Him. Even the very hairs of our head are numbered, and not one sparrow falls to the ground without His knowledge (Mt. 10:21-31). Let God be your friend in every area of your life. He is interested in your salvation, your health, your business, and in all the things you are concerned about. Do all you can and leave the rest with God.

Grounds for Asking and Receiving

The true grounds for prayer and its answer is to be born again and have the right relationship to God. Only true, saved men have the right to ask and receive anything that they want from God. Sinners who rebel and refuse to surrender their lives to God and become reconciled to Him have no true grounds of approach to God except to repent. They have no foundation for their faith except promises of forgiveness. God, many times in His mercy, helps sinners and hears their cries of despair, but He is not obligated to do for them what He has promised His children until they obey Him. It is merely because He wants to prove His love and mercy to the sinner, and show him that even though He is a rebel, God sometimes hears the cries of a sinner. Paul said, "the goodness of

God leadeth thee to repentance" and "God commendeth His love toward us, in that, while we were yet sinners Christ died for us" (Rom. 2:4; 5:8).

What Sinners Can Legally Claim

The first promise that a sinner can legally claim through the death of Christ is that of forgiveness and cleansing from sin (Acts 2:38; 3:19; 1 Jn. 1:9). If a sinner will truly repent and turn from sin, he is immediately on "praying grounds" for anything else that God has promised to men. So a right relationship with God is the true foundation for asking and receiving (Mt. 7:7-11; Lk. 11:1-13; Jn. 14:12-15; 15:7, 16; 16:23-26; 1 Jn. 3:20-24; 5:13-15).

Asking and Receiving are Personal Rights of God's Children

With the proper relationship to God it becomes our family right, our legal right, our redemptive right, our gospel right, our needful right and our creative right to ask and receive anything and everything that the Father has promised His own children. There should be no question about personal rights or the outcome of prayer according to those rights, for all things belong to God and His children, and His sons will inherit all things in the end when rebellion is put down (Rom. 8:17-18; 1 Pet. 1:2-5). If all things belong to us and we will finally inherit them, why not get what we want of them here and now? Why should it not be our right to get everything that God has promised we can have in this life?

Jesus taught us that children of God have a right to get *all* their prayers answered. When the Gentile woman came to Jesus to get her daughter healed, Jesus answered, "It is not meet to take the children's bread, and cast it to the dogs" (Mt. 15:21-26). She answered wisely and asked for only the "crumbs" that are the right of a dog. He could not resist her faith and said, "O woman, great is thy faith: be it unto thee even as thou wilt; and her daughter was made whole from that very hour." This certainly teaches that children of God have certain rights in the heavenly family. They have just as much right to expect good things from God as any child in an earthly family has a right to expect things from his parents. At least one has the rights of a dog if not the rights of a child, so let us have at least the faith of a dog if not the faith of a child.

The Certainty of Answered Prayer

Asking is receiving according to Jesus: "Ask, and it shall be given you; seek, and ye shall find; knock, and it shall be opened unto you: for every one that asketh *receiveth*; and he that seeketh *findeth*; and to him that knocketh *it shall be opened*" (Mt. 7:7-8). The first letters of these three words: "ask," "seek," and "knock," spell *ask*. This is not a mere coincidence. It is a divine fact that all one has to do is to ask. Asking, however, presupposes a God who hears and answers prayers. If one asks in mockery or from mere form without faith, he does not truly ask. One must ask in faith, nothing wavering, and then he will receive (Jas. 1:5-8; Heb. 11:6). There can be no failure, or God is not true; so let there not be one doubt about it, for God is true. The certainty of answered prayer, unlimited promises for asking and receiving, as well as the infinite possibilities in prayer are found in the Scriptures above under Point 2.

The certainty of answered prayer is also expressed in the Old Testament: "The eyes of the Lord are upon the righteous, and his ears are open unto their cry. The righteous cry, and the Lord heareth, and delivereth them out of all their troubles" (Ps. 34:15-17); "Delight thyself also in the Lord; and he shall give thee the desires of thine heart. Commit thy way unto the Lord; trust also in him; and he shall bring it to pass" (Ps. 37:4-5); "He shall call upon me, and I will answer him: I will be with him in trouble; I will deliver him, and honour him" (Ps. 91:15); "No good thing will he withhold from them that walk uprightly" (Ps. 84:11).

God Loves His Children More Than Do Earthly Parents

Jesus taught the infinite fatherhood of God and stated that God loves His children more than any human parent could possibly love his own flesh and blood. This means that it is not and cannot be the will of God for any child of His to be sinful, rebellious, defeated, unhappy, sick, poor, wanting, worrying, complaining, or discouraged. It could not be the will of earthly parents for their children to suffer these things, and no parent would tolerate these conditions in the lives of their children if they could help it. Earthly parents would speedily deliver their children from all such enemies if they could. Earthly parents long to help and will do everything possible to help their children obtain the best things in life, to be healthy, to be prosperous, and happy. Does God love His children any less than do earthly parents? Certainly not!

Jesus proved that God loves His children more than earthly parents when He said, "Or what man is there of you, whom if his son ask bread, will he give him a stone? Or if be ask a fish, will he give him a serpent? If ye then being evil, know how to give good gifts unto your children, *how much more* shall your heavenly Father which is in heaven give good things to them that *ask* him?" (Mt. 7:9-11). What more could a child of God want than such a broad, all–inclusive promise of the infinite fatherhood of God. What more could one desire for proof that it is the will of God for him to ask anything—wealth, health, cleansing from sin, keeping from sin, or anything that one desires?

Answers to Prayer the Will of God

In the same sermon on the mount Jesus taught us to pray, "Thy will be done in earth, *as it is in heaven*" (Mt. 6:10). Is it God's will for men to be sick and sinful when they get to Heaven? Is it God's will for men to be defeated and poverty–stricken and unhappy in Heaven? Is it God's will for men to be tormented by demons and to carry about forever in Heaven the works of the devil in their bodies, souls, and spirits? Is it God's will in Heaven for men to be abandoned by God and forsaken by Him after He once gets them there? You know the answer to these questions! If these things are not God's will in Heaven, they are not God's will on Earth. We can have freedom from these things on Earth just as much as we will be free from them in Heaven if we will but *ask and receive*, according to the will of God, here and now. Now is the time we need to ask and receive—not in the next life. Here and now we need the will of God done and not only in Heaven, for we are not yet there.

Chapter Eleven

SCRIPTURAL PROOF FOR DIVINE HEALING

It is a constant experience in our ministry to hear men and women, seeking God for healing of the body, question the will of God for healing. Multiplied thousands of Christians pray daily for deliverance from sickness and pain by saying, "If it be thy will." And, unfortunately, this is the reason why tens of thousands of cases are not healed by God in answer to prayer. Such a prayer is not "the prayer of faith," nor is it in harmony with the revealed will of God. In fact, it is a prayer contrary to the will of God. It is a prayer of unbelief. Every time we state this we are met by a wide range of arguments fro people who maintain that such a prayer is the proper way to pray. They will listen neither to reason nor to the Scriptures, and so they go without the benefits of healing provided in the atonement and promised by God in His Word.

In the next four chapters we propose to prove from Scripture that it is the will of God for every child of His to have freedom from all sickness, pain, disease, and physical suffering for which Jesus died to deliver them from in this life. It is God's will for His children to have power over these things and to be in sound health all their days.

What Divine Healing and Health is Not

Diving healing is not healing and health by natural remedies, imagination, will power, personal magnetism, metaphysics, demonology, spiritualism, immunity from death, presumption, insubordination to God's will, mind over matter, denial of the plain facts of sin, sickness, and disease, or natural healing by natural laws.

What Divine Healing and Health Is

Divine healing and health is a definite act of God through faith in Jesus by the power of the Holy Spirit, the Word of God, and the precious blood of Christ, whereby the human body is cured, healed, repaired, delivered from sickness and its power, and made as whole, sound, and healthy as it was before the attack.

Eighty Scriptural Arguments for Divine Healing

There are eighty reasons for believing in the healing of the body that we shall list together with many Scriptures that prove each point.

The Bible plainly teaches:

(1)   That divine healing for the body is scriptural (Mt. 8: 17; 1 Pet. 2:24).
(2)   That health was natural before sin entered (Gen. 1:26-31; 2:17).
(3)   That death entered through sin as part of the curse (Rom. 5:12-21).

(4) That the first prophecy and promise of redemption included healing for the body through Jesus Christ (Gen. 3:15; Isa. 53:5; Mt. 8:16-17; 1 Pet. 2:24).

(5) That sickness originated with sin and is now being propagated by Satan and demons (Job 2:6-7; Mt. 4: 23-24; 15:22; 17:14-21; Lk. 13:16; Jn. 10:10; Acts 10:38).

(6) That the first recorded healing in Scripture was through prayer (Gen. 20:7, 17).

(7) That the first recorded bodily affliction was the consequence of disobeying God and that when conditions were met, healing was given in answer to prayer (Gen. 20:1-18).

(8) That in all cases of healing in Scripture, prayer, atonement, and spiritual means were used instead of human remedies (Gen. 20:7, 17; Ex. 15:26; Ps. 103:1-4; 105:37; 107:20; Acts 10:38; Jas. 5:14-16; 1 Pet. 2:24; Mt. 8:17).

(9) That spiritual means to heal sicknesses and diseases is all that God has provided for man (Ex. 15:26; Mt. 8:16-17; Jas. 5:14; 1 Pet. 2:24).

(10) That spiritual means is all that God has promised and commanded to be used in sickness (Jas. 5:14-16; Ex. 15:26; Ps. 91; Mt. 8:16-17; 1 Pet. 2:24).

(11) That God cursed His people who did not trust Him in sickness and disease (2 Ki. 1; 2 Chr. 16:12-14; Jer. 17:5-10).

(12) That there is no case recorded in Scripture where men received benefits from any other source than by spiritual means (Ps. 103:1-4; 107:20; Mt. 8:17; 1 Pet. 2:24).

(13) That multitudes have been healed by spiritual means (Ps. 105:20; Acts 10:38).

(14) That no Scripture encourages human remedies to cure disease (Mt. 8:17; 1 Pet. 2:24).

(15) That Bible characters used spiritual means in times of sickness (Ps. 38; 103:1-3; 107:20; Jas. 5:14-16; 1 Pet. 2:24; Mt. 8:17).

(16) That God made a covenant with His people to heal them (Ex. 15:26; 23:23; Lev. 26; Dt. 7:15; 28:1-65; Jas. 5:14-16; Mt. 8:16-17; 1 Pet. 2:24).

(17) That God kept His part of the covenant (Ps. 103:1-4; 105:37; 107:20; Mt. 8:17).

(18) That only spiritual means were used by Israel in the wilderness (Ex. 15:26; 32:7-28; Num. 11:1-3; 12: 13-16; 21:1-9; Jn. 3:14; Ps. 105:37; 107:20).

(19) That healing was promised on condition of obedience to God (Lev. 26; Dt. 28; Ex. 15:26; Ps. 91; 107: 17-21).

(20) That the brazen serpent, a type of Christ, caused healing (Num. 21:1-9; Jn. 3:14). Should we expect less of Christ, the antitype, than from the type of Christ? (Jn. 10:10).

(21) That healing always came unless certain ones had sinned and were under the curse of the law, which had to be upheld (Lev. 10; Num. 11:19-20; 25:1-14).

(22) That the heathen outside the covenants of God were not promised healing until they came under the terms of the covenants and lived up to them (Ex. 15:26).

(23) That all the plagues upon Israel occurred because of sin (Lev. 26; Dt. 28).

(24) That eleven out of thirteen plagues upon Israel in the wilderness were caused by the misuse of the tongue (Ex. 15:24-26; 32:1-6; Num. 11, 12, 13, 14, 16 and 21).

(25) That God did permit the devil to afflict Job, but that God used the affliction to purify and refine him (Job 2:6-7; 42:1-7). God did not leave him sick all of his life; so this is no example to prove that modern believers should remain sick. After the test God healed him; so if anyone today claims he is under a test like Job, let him also learn his lesson and receive healing. Let him believe God will heal him as He did Job.

(26) That God, to bring sinners to repentance, does permit Satan to afflict them (Job 33:12-30; 1 Cor. 5: 1-5; 2 Cor. 2:6-11).

(27) That God always healed when the lessons were learned and men came to repentance (Gen. 20:7, 17; Num. 11:2; 12:13-16; 21:1-9; Job 33:12-30; 42: 1-12; Ps. 103:3; Jas. 5:14-16).

(28) That God permits Satan to afflict His people when they go astray (Ps. 38; 103:3; Num. 12:13-16; 21: 1-9; Gal. 6:7-8).

(29) That bodily healing is taught in both Testaments, in every division of the books of the Bible, and in almost every book of the Bible, as seen in the Scriptures in the points above and below.

(30) That sickness is the only means God can use to wake some men to their need of God and bring them to repentance (Job 33:12-30; Hos. 6:1).

(31) That divine health as well as divine healing was promised when certain conditions were met (Lev. 26; Dt. 28; Ex. 15:26; Ps. 91; Pr. 3:1-8; 12:18; 13:3; 15:4; 18:8, 21; Isa. 58; Jas. 5:14-16; 1 Pet. 3:10-11; 3 Jn. 2).

(32) That Christ came to redeem from both sin and sickness (Isa. 53; 61:1-2; Mt. 8:16-17; 9:1-10; Gal. 3:13;

Rom. 8:11; Acts 10:38; 1 Pet. 2:24; 1 Jn. 3:8).

(33) That healing is in fulfillment of prophecy (Isa. 35: 1-12; 53:1-12; 61:1-2; Mt. 8:16-17; Acts 10:38; 1 Pet. 2:24).

(34) That Jesus proved His claims to sonship by healing men (Mt. 4:23-24; 11:3-6; Lk. 4:18-25; 13:32, 33; Acts 10:38; 1 Jn. 3:8).

(35) That Jesus authorized the twelve to heal as they went preaching (Mt. 10).

(36) That He also authorized the seventy to heal as they preached (Lk. 10).

(37) That the disciples were successful in healing and casting out devils before Pentecost (Mt. 10; Lk. 10; Mk. 6:7-13).

(38) That the disciples were authorized to carry on the work of healing throughout this age to confirm the Word of God (Mt. 28:20; Heb. 2:3-4; Mk. 16:17-20).

(39) That the early believers confirmed the Word by healing (Mk. 16:20; Acts 2:43; 3:1-12; 5:12-16; 6:8; 8:7-13; 11:19-22; 14:3, 27; 15:4, 12; 19:11-12; 28:9; Rom. 15:18-19, 29; 1 Cor. 16:10; Heb. 2:3-4).

(40) That all disciples throughout this age are commanded to observe all things Christ commanded the early disciples (Mt. 28:20; Acts 1:1-8).

(41) That Jesus commanded the disciples to get definite power to confirm the Word of God before they went out (Lk. 24:49; Acts 1:1-8; Mk. 16:15-20; Jn. 14: 12-15).

(42) That Jesus sent the Holy Spirit into the world to carry on the healing ministry that He had started (Acts 1:1-8; 2:33-34; 1 Cor. 12:7-11; Heb. 2:3-4; Jn. 14:12).

(43) That Jesus promised such power to every believer (Mk. 9:23; 11:22-24; 16:15-20; Jn. 14:12-15; 15:7, 16).

(44) That the gifts of healing are part of the spiritual equipment of the church (1 Cor. 1:7; 12:11; Rom. 12:6-8; 15:18-19, 29; Heb. 2:3-4).

(45) That healing is part of the church work (Jas. 5:14-16; Cor. 12:1-11).

(46) That it is always God's will to heal His children in the New Covenant (Mt. 6:10; 7:7-11; 8:3, 7, 16-17; Mk. 9:23; 11:22-24; 16:15-20; Jn. 14:12-15; 15:7, 16; 16:23-26; Heb. 11:6; Jas. 1:5-9; 5:14-16).

(47) That healing is in the atonement (Isa. 53:4-5; Mt. 8:16-17; 1 Pet. 2:24; 1 Cor. 11:23-32; Jn. 3:14; Jas. 5:14-16; 3 Jn. 2).

(48) That apart from the atonement God would have no right to answer prayer for healing, for death was the penalty for sin and the law must be upheld; the sinner would have no right to ask God for healing, for he is under the death sentence; Christ would not have healed, for there would have been no means of forgiveness and healing; He would not have authorized His ministers to carry on His work; the Spirit would have no basis for working among men; and none of the penalty for sin or the results of sin could be done away with (Mt. 8:17; 1 Pet. 2:21).

(49) That healing is part of the children's bread and their right by virtue of redemption (Mt. 7:7-11; 15:22-28; Mk. 7:29; Lk. 13:16; Jn. 3:14-16; 14:12-15; 15:7, 16; 16:23-26; 1 Jn. 3:8, 20-22; 5:14-15; 3 Jn. 2).

(50) That healing is part of the work of the Holy Spirit in believers (Rom. 8:11; 1 Cor. 12:7-11; Heb. 2:3-4; Acts 1:8; Lk. 24:49).

(51) That failure to appropriate healing by faith in the broken body and shed blood of Christ frequently has resulted in premature death (1 Cor. 11:23-32).

(52) That healing proves that one has the Holy Spirit in him (Rom. 8:11; 1 Cor. 12).

(53) That healing proves that one is a full–fledged believer in all the truth of the gospel (Jn. 14:12; Mk. 16:15-20).

(54) That healing proves that Jesus Christ lives today (Heb. 13:8; Jn. 14:12).

(55) That healing proves that the individual has exercised faith and has claimed and received his redemptive rights (Mk. 11:22-24; 16:15-20; Jn. 14:12-25; 15:7, 16; 16:23-26; Heb. 11:6; Jas. 1:5-9; 5:14-16).

(56) That healing is one of the signs that were to follow believers (Mk. 16:15-20).

(57) That healing is in God's plan for this age as well as in the Millennium (Mk. 16:15-20; Jn. 14:12-15; Isa. 30:26; 33:24; 35:1-10).

(58) That healing proves that God's promises are true (2 Pet. 1:4-5; Jas. 5:14-16; Rom. 8:11; Mk. 11:22-24; Jn. 14:12-15; 15:7, 16; 2 Cor. 1:20).

(59) That because full instructions on how to get healed and stay healed are carefully given in Scripture, healing must be the will of God, and that such benefits will be realized if instructions are followed (Isa. 58:1-14; Jer. 17:5-10; Ps. 34:12-13; 37:1-8; 91:1-12; 103:1-3; Ex. 15:26; Lev. 26; Dt. 28; Pr. 3:1-8; 12:18; 13:3; 15:4; 18:8, 21; Mt. 7:7-11; 17:14-21; 21:21; Mk. 9:23; 11:22-24; 16:15-20; Jn. 14:12-15; 15:7, 16; 16:23-26; Rom. 4:17; Heb. 11:6; Jas. 1:5-9; 4:7; 5:14-16).

(60) That healing is included in our salvation, for the

Hebrew and Greek words for "salvation" imply the ideas of *healing, health, preservation,* and *soundness* (Rom. 1:16).

(61) That healing is to be expected as a manifestation of the fatherhood, love, and will of God for His children as it would be of any earthly parent (Mt. 6:10; 7:7-11; Mk. 9:23; 11:22-24; Lk. 11:1-13; 18:1-18; Jn. 14:12-15; 15:7, 16; 16:23-26; Heb. 11:6; Jas. 1:5-9; 5:14-16). Is God the only father who desires that His children be always sick and diseased? Is He the only one who does not love His children? Is He the only one who would prefer His children to have weaknesses, failures, sins, sicknesses, material wants, and constant defeat by their enemy? Does He love His children less than earthly parents? Is He the only one who is a respecter of persons and will heal one and not another, will help men in one age and not in another, will provide healing for some and not for others, and will love and benefit some of His children but not all others? Is He the only father who promises unlimited benefits for His children and then refuses to give them such blessings when they are needed? No! A thousand times No! God loves His children and wills for them the best, as any true father does, and He will always give His children what He has promised and what they want if they will have faith in Him.

(62) That healing is the natural result of meeting certain conditions, and that all the powers of darkness cannot keep a believer sick if and when these conditions are met (Isa. 58; Pr. 3:1-8; 12:18; 13:3; 15:4; 18:8, 21; Ps. 34:12-13; 1 Pet. 3:10; Heb. 11:6; Jas. 1:5-9; 4:7; 5:14-16; Mk. 11:22-24; Jn. 14:12-15; 15:7, 16).

(63) That healing is on the same basis as forgiveness of sins and is just as easy to obtain (Mt. 9:1-7; 13:15; Acts 8:27; Jas. 5:14-16).

(64) That healing proves the resurrection of Christ (Rom. 8:11; Acts 3:15-16).

(65) That healing is one of the best means of attracting men to the gospel (Jn. 6:2; Acts 3:1-11; 5:12-16; 6:8; 8:1-20; 9:32-42; 14:8-16, 27; 15:4, 12; 19:11-20).

(66) That healing is one of the quickest ways of getting men converted (Jn. 4:46-53; 11:45; Acts 4:4; 5:12-16; 8:5-8; 9:34-35; 19:11-20; 28:4-10).

(67) That healing is the best means of glorifying God (Mk. 2:12; Lk. 13:17; Acts 3:8). How can people who are defeated and held in bondage by the work of Satan be free to glorify God for permitting them to stay in bondage? How can people glorify God for the work of the devil in them? How can God's work be carried forward when God's people are defeated and helpless?

(68) That healing and health is a personal choice just like forgiveness of sins and personal salvation (Mt. 7:7-11; Mk. 11:22-24; Heb. 11:6; Jas. 1:5-9; 4:7; 5:14).

(69) That there is no excuse for children of God to be sick and defeated by Satan, for all things are possible to him that believeth (Mk. 9:23; 11:22-24; Jn. 15:7, 16).

(70) That it is God's highest will and wish for His children to be happy, healthy, and prosperous (3 Jn. 2; Ps. 1:2-3; Mk. 11:22-24; Jn. 15:7, 16; Mt. 7:7-11).

(71) That if Satan has the power to bring all kinds of diseases upon men, he also has the power to remove them if he can get men to follow some unbiblical religion that will eventually damn the soul (Mt.

7:21-23; 24:24; 2 Cor. 11:13-15; 2 Th. 2:8-12; Rev. 12:9; 13:2, 13). A number of false religions that deny such essentials of the gospel as the blood of Christ, His bodily resurrection, salvation from sin through the blood, and others, are claiming healings and material benefits for their followers. This cannot be doubted, but such benefits should not be accepted from this source, for it is the work of Satan to get men to deny the gospel that will save the soul. One should reject these benefits from Satan and seek and receive them from God, and then no part of the gospel will have to be rejected.

(72) That Satan cannot touch God's people without permission from their Heavenly Father; so if everyone will walk in truth as he receives it, there will be no permission given (1 Cor. 11:29-32; 1 Jn. 1:7; Ps. 91).

(73) That God's people, if they live clean and holy lives, can enjoy long life without being sick (Ps. 91; 3 Jn. 2; 1 Jn. 1:7; Eph. 6:2; 1 Pet. 3:10).

(74) That God has provided all necessary weapons to defeat sin, sickness, and all the works of Satan (2 Cor. 10:4-5; Eph. 6:10-18; Mk. 16:15-20; Jn. 14: 12-15; 15:7, 16; Gal. 5:16-22; Rom. 8:1-39; Jas. 4: 7; 5:14-16; 1 Pet. 5:8-9).

(75) That God's program of healing is the same today as much as ever (Jn. 14:12-15; 15:7, 16; Mk. 16:15-20; Acts 1:1-8). The devil is the same. His works are the same. His power in the lives of men needs to be broken today as ever. God is the same. His works and will are the same. His power is still available for believers to destroy the works of the devil. The only thing remaining for the church is to

awake to its rightful place in the gospel and launch a Hell–defeating campaign by getting back to New Testament living and power. Believers should ask God for the power He gave the early church (Lk. 24:49; Acts 1:8; Jude 3); carry out the great commission to the letter (Mt. 28:19-20; Mk. 16:15-20; Acts 1:8); keep the commandments of Christ (Jn. 14:12-15; 15:10-17); follow Christ in speaking and working (Jn. 5:19, 30; 8:28-29; 12:49; 14:10-12) and in living (1 Jn. 2:6; 3:7; 4:17; 1 Pet. 2:21); walk in the Spirit (Gal. 5:16-24); put to death all carnal traits contrary to the will of God (Rom. 8:1-13; Col. 3:5-17); and practice literally the gospel of the New Testament as it reads, not as we interpret it to read. When believers begin to do these things they will again see New Testament power and experiences.

(76) That the gospel is still the power of God unto salvation (Rom. 1:16). Healing is included in salvation, for this word means "deliverance," "healing," "soundness" and "preservation for body, soul, and spirit" (Lk. 1:69-71; 18:42).

(77) That sickness will not come upon God's people unless they turn from holiness to sin (Ex. 15:26; Lev. 26; Dt. 28), or unless they give in to demon attacks (Eph. 6:10-18; Jas. 4:7). If this was true of preservation from sickness in the Old Covenant, it is much more true of men under the New Covenant, which contains greater promises and a greater glory than the old one did (2 Cor. 3:6-15; Heb. 7:22; 8:6). In Psalm 91 we have a whole chapter which promises immunity from sickness, and this applies to the New Covenant times as well as to the Old Covenant period. In Isaiah 58 we have another chapter prom-

ising divine health, providing we do the twenty things listed in this Scripture.

(78) That sickness is never the will of God for His people. Believers in the New Covenant have the privilege to ask "what ye will" (Jn. 15:7); "whatsoever" (Mt. 21:21; Jn. 14:13; 15:16; 16:23-26; 1 Jn. 3:22; 5:14-15); "anything" (Jn. 14:14; Mt. 18: 18-20); "what things soever ye desire" (Mk. 11:22-24), and "much more" than earthly parents would or could give their children" (Mt. 7:7-11). What could be more all–inclusive and unlimited than these promises? What could express the highest will of God more than these? What could be more definite than these to prove that "all things are possible to him that believeth?" (Mt. 17:20; Mk. 9:23). If then it is left up to the will of each believer to get what he wills, and if it is God's will for each one to get what he wills, then why should anyone will to be sick when he can will otherwise if he chooses? He will be in the perfect will of God by so doing. He will be healed.

(79) That God answers prayer even after judgment has been pronounced upon the sick one (Isa. 38; Num. 14:12-20; Ex. 32:10-14).

(80) That healing demonstrates the power of God over the power of Satan (Acts 10:38; 26:18; 1 Jn. 3:8; Lk. 13:16; Jn. 10:10). Dealing with sickness, then, should be on the same basis as dealing with sin and Satan. If one will recognize the true source of his troubles and that God desires to heal—and that He will heal if He is asked to do so in faith—he will get a speedy deliverance from the enemy of both God and man. As long as men think it is God's will for them to be sick

and that God is causing the trouble, then they believe lies and the truth cannot set them free. God moves within His own laws and He will not work because of unbelief; because of the refusal of the sick one to clear God of all guilt for his trouble; because of belief in lies instead of truth; because of cooperation with Satan instead of with God; and because of the exercise of unbelief instead of faith. God works only upon the principles of faith and truth, and He will not break His Word for any person (Heb. 11:6; Jas. 1:5-9; Jn. 8:21-32).

These eighty lessons must be learned, and the truth must be obeyed, and faith must be exercised *without wavering* before God is obligated to deliver any sick person from the hands of the devil. If you are sick it will pay you to meditate upon the above eighty lessons gleaned from a study of the Scriptures and from over 100 Bible cases of sickness. You can be healed instantly when you believe the truth. It will automatically set you free (Jn. 8:31-32). Do not live in ignorance and unbelief any longer. Do not be satisfied with defeat. Take an aggressive stand against sin, unbelief, sickness, and Satan, and all the demons out of Hell cannot hold you in bondage. Jesus loves you and has come to set you free; so believe it and yield to Him for the deliverance. He said, "The thief cometh not, but for to steal, and to kill, and to destroy: I am come *that they might have life, and that they might have it more abundantly*" (Jn. 10:10).

Chapter Twelve

UNBELIEF ANSWERED WITH SCRIPTURE

There are a number of excuses for unbelief that are regularly used by those who seek healing of the body and answers to prayer from God. Such excuses are the reason why tens of thousands of people do not obtain healing or see their prayers answered. Jesus said, "Ye shall know the truth, and the truth shall make you free" (Jn. 8:32). It is by truth that we are set free and it is by lies and fallacies that we are bound by the devil and demons. It is important therefore that those who want freedom know the truth that sets free. The Psalmist said, "He sent his word, and healed them, and delivered them from their destructions . . . and there was not one feeble person in all their tribes" (Ps. 107:20; 105:37). The centurion said, "Speak the word only and my servant shall be healed" (Mt. 8:8). It is said of Jesus that "He cast out the spirits with His word, and healed all that were sick" (Mt. 8:16-17). It was the Word that Jesus preached to the people that healed them (Mk. 2:2). It was the Word that God confirmed by healing the sick when the apostles preached it (Mk. 16:17-20). It was the Word that brought life and cleansing from sin and disease in the disciples (Jn. 4:50; 5:24; 6:63; 8:31-37; 15:3, 7; 17:17). The gospel is the power of God unto salvation to everyone that believeth (Rom. 1:16). Salvation includes healing of the body (Mt. 9:1-8; 13:15; Acts 3:16; 4:12; 28:27; Jas. 5:14-16). *Note the following excuses for unbelief that Christians freely use that rob them of the things they need from God:*

That People are Sick for God's Glory

A very common excuse for unbelief is that some people are sick for God's glory. The favorite Scriptures that demons use to persuade men that they are sick for the glory of God are John 9:1-3 and 11:4. It is argued that the blind man and Lazarus in these Scriptures were sick and afflicted for the glory of God and that it must have been the will of God for them to be this way or it would not have happened to them.

Naturally, God cannot receive glory from healing if no one is ever sick, but the fact that God heals is no proof that sickness and disease is His will. Think about it—if it were the will of God for people to be sick, then He never would have healed anyone to oppose His own will. God never would have sent Jesus to heal all the sick against the will of God if it were His will for them to be sick. The reason God healed was to prove to men that it was not His will for them to be sick. The glory God received out of all the cases of healing in Scripture was not in the sicknesses, but in the healings. If the blind man had remained blind, or if Lazarus had remained sick or dead, God would not have been glorified. The devil would have been glorified, for his work would have continued to be manifest in them. No person can glorify God and magnify His work until it is manifest in Him. This should stir every child of God to refuse such deception any longer—the deception of being sick for the glory of God.

It is the devil that causes the sickness—and then he tries to make the sick one believe that God is responsible and that it is God's will for him to be sick. As long as the deceived one thinks he is glorifying God and that he is in accord with the will of God by being sick, let him never seek to get well by prayer, doctors, medicines, or by any other means. On the contrary, let him desire to become more sick in order to glorify God all the more and in order to get deeper in the will of God! No one can conscientiously believe such an idea, but some think it convenient to accuse God of the work of Satan as an excuse for their unbelief.

Suppose a rich man in a community would promise to pay all hospital bills and buy new cars for all who got into a serious accident. Suppose there were a number of accidents; should he be accused of deliberately causing them just because he promised to help men out of their troubles? Should he be accused of causing them in order to receive praise for helping his neighbors? It is true that his goodness would be magnified by such acts of kindness, but his kindness would not be the cause of the wrecks. He would not desire the accidents, and he would prevent them if at all possible. If he deliberately caused the wrecks in order to get praise for helping those who were injured, all would rise up to destroy him and reject such benevolence.

So it is with God. Men get into sin and sickness, or they are attacked by satanic powers, and God helps them out of their troubles, thereby receiving the glory due Him for His goodness. This does not prove that

God wills the affliction or that He is the cause of the trouble. It is simply the fact that God gets glory in spite of them, not because He is responsible for them. God gets no glory out of any sickness as long as the sick one remains that way. He only receives glory from healing when He can get men to believe and be healed.

That Sickness is the Chastening of God

This argument is that the sick one is under the chastening of God and that it would be presumptuous to ask God to heal under such circumstances. We answer by saying that it is *never* presumptuous to pray for those blessings that are abundantly promised by God and that are provided for in the atonement. Many Scriptures promise healing, as we have seen above in Chapter Eleven. Healing is provided for in the atonement, as we have also seen and shall see more fully below. Therefore, it could not possibly be wrong to pray with divine assurance for healing if all the conditions are met. It is the will of God to heal or He would not have made such promises or made such provision on Calvary. It is presumptuous to doubt God and have unbelief in His Word and provision. It is presumptuous to pray in such a doubtful and unbelieving state or to ask in any other spirit than that of confident expectation for what is provided for us in the gospel.

One of God's eternal names confirming an eternal covenant of healing was revealed to Moses in Ex. 15:26. It was *Jehovah-Raphah*, "I *am* the Lord that healeth thee." This was the faith of the Psalmist when he said, "Who forgiveth all thine iniquities; who healeth all thy diseases" (Ps. 103:1-4). This name is as unchangeable as God Himself. It reveals the nature of God as the healer of His people. His promises are in perfect accord with the revelation of Himself.

Christ is God's way of healing His people. The prophet predicted the work of Christ as the healer of men (Isa 53:1-12). Christ's ministry was made up of preaching and healing (Mt. 4:23-24; 9:35; Acts 10:38). Christ healed the people that prophecy might be fulfilled (Mt. 8:16-17; 1 Pet. 2:24). The New Testament books and all church history reveal the work of God in healing His people in all ages. God is now sending a revival of healing to the world and multitudes are being healed.

In our office we have numerous testimonies of healing and answered prayer. People have been healed through reading the fifty-two Bible lesson course, *God's Plan for Man*, and by laying hands on the radio as we pray for the people. We have testimonies of people being healed of throat trouble, kidney and bladder trouble, broken bones, stomach trouble, ulcers of the stomach, cancer, nervousness, heart trouble, fevers, arthritis, blood poisoning, deafness, skin diseases, colitis, insanity, tuberculosis, paralysis, and many other sicknesses and diseases. We have testimonies of people being delivered from sin, whiskey, tobacco, dope, and bad habits of all kinds. Financial problems have been solved. Work has been found and prayers for many blessings of life have been answered.

The Greek word for "chastening" in Heb. 12:5-10 is *paideuo* and means "child training." It is translated: "instructing" (2 Tim. 2:25); "taught" (Acts 22:3); "teaching" (Titus 2:12); "learn" (1 Tim. 1:20); "learned" (Acts

7:22); "chastened" (1 Cor. 11:32; 2 Cor 6:9; Heb.12:5-10; Rev. 3:19); and "chastise" (Lk. 23:16, 22). It is clear from these passages that chastening does not always mean "to make one sick." This is not the only way God chastens, as is clear in the Scriptures above and by the way the word is used in the Old Testament (2 Sam. 7:14; Pr. 19:18; Ps. 73:14).

Suppose we should conclude that a child cannot be chastened or educated unless he is made sick. When you send a child to college do you say, "Now, Mr. Smith, I send you my child to educate him. Be sure to see that he gets a regular dose of disease every month. Give him tuberculosis, cancer, tumors, typhoid fever, polio, small pox, and the worst kind of chastening possible in order to correct and educate him. I want him to have the best education possible, so give him all the diseases you can. Be sure and break a leg or two during the term and knock out an eye if he needs correction. Show him the best love possible. Chasten him as the Lord does His children: for whom the Lord loveth he *maketh sick*." That's ridiculous!

It is a known fact that disease and calamities do not, in every case, bring men any closer to God. They more often drive men to hate God and backslide because they think God is responsible. It is the Holy Spirit and the *goodness of God* that draw men closer to God. Suppose we say to you that we have a choice stock of diseases and calamities and we want to demonstrate how much we love you. Suppose we say, "Come here and let us give you a dozen cancers that will eat your body and cause unbearable pain. Let us give you several diseases at once so that we can emphasize our love to you. Or let us cut off your arms and legs and cut out your eyes as we have a special love for you." You would say, "if that is the kind of love you have for me then please keep it to yourself. I do not want that kind of love." You say this reasoning is the most ridiculous kind that I have ever heard. You must be insane to talk that way. Yes, such love would be criminal and the acts of maniacs, yet this is the kind of wonderful, infinite, and gentle love some men accuse God of having. "Whom the Lord loveth, He chasteneth" is quoted many thousands of times in connection with sick Christians. As a last resort God will deal harshly with rebels and permit Satan to attack them (Job 33:14-30), but Christians can be immune from sickness (Ex. 15:26; Ps. 84:11; 91:1-12; Isa. 58; Mk. 11:22-24; Jn. 14:12-15; 15:7, 16; 3 Jn. 2).

You say, "Such is permitted of God or it would not happen." Yes, we will agree with you that it is permitted, but only in the sense that He does not definitely intervene to stop men from committing crimes, destroy themselves, or whatever they do because of sin. God will permit every one of you to jump in front of an automobile, or jump off a cliff to kill yourself if that is what you want to do. He will permit you to take poison or shoot yourself. He permits men to do all things that they do simply because He does not forcibly stop them.

Again, you may say that God teaches men many lessons through sickness and calamity. That may be true, but He never *causes* men to get into these troubles in order to teach him these lessons. *He could have taught them the same lessons without men getting into these troubles.* If my son gets into trouble I will naturally use this as an occasion to teach him certain lessons and make a better man out of him, but I would be wicked if I caused him to get into these troubles just to teach him certain lessons. So it is with God. He helps men learn things in *spite* of suffering, not *because* of it.

The sick one hides behind Hebrews 12:5-10, but this passage compares the chastening of God to that of human parents, and we know that no human parent will chasten any child by sickness and disease. Is God less loving than earthly parents? Jesus taught that He was *more* loving than men; so if men will not chasten by such means, then *lay this theory aside and quit being deceived by Satan!* All the sick one has to do is to recognize that the source of his trouble is the devil and then cooperate with God to defeat him so that healing will come, and then God will receive the glory (Jn. 10:10; Acts 10:38).

If men will not obey God or exercise faith in Him and offer resistance to Satan, then God will not work on their behalf. A good father will help a boy get out of trouble, but he will never be responsible for getting him into it. A father will use the occasion of the troubles his children get into to teach certain lessons and perhaps chastise them, but he will not deliberately be a party to the destruction of his children. A good father will also help rescue a child when he is attacked and beaten by an enemy, but he will never jump on the boy and help his enemy destroy him.

Likewise, a child of God does not have to accept sickness as a chastening from God. He needs to realize he is set upon by demons and not by God, that if he has sinned this gave demons the occasion to attack, and that God is the source of his deliverance. Only one passage on chastening in the New Testament could be used of physical sickness, and the cause of the failure to get healing here is *not appropriating healing from the broken body and the shed blood of Christ*, not the chastening of God. So the law of sowing and reaping had to be executed (1 Cor. 11:27-32). They could have believed God instead of being defeated through unbelief. They merely reaped what they sowed and this will *always* be the law of God (Gal. 6:7-8).

When one says he is under the chastening of God, he admits that he has sinned and rebelled against God to the point where he got into the hands of Satan, and therefore, he thinks that God will do nothing except permit him to reap what he has sowed. But in the circumstances he can still repent and surrender to God who will immediately heal him if he will have faith (Job 33:14-29; Ps. 38 and 61). Where no known sin has been committed—and yet a sick one imagines they must be ill because of something that they have done—demonic deception and attack is clearly the case, and should be met by a vigorous resistance in the name of Jesus and by faith in the blood of Christ (Jas. 4:7; 1 Pet. 5:8-9).

That God is the One Who Sends Afflictions

We have already seen in Chapter Eleven that Satan is the cause of afflictions. The third excuse for unbelief is that God is the one who does the afflicting, so why ask him to remove it? Christians hide behind this excuse because David said, "Many are the afflictions of the righteous" (Ps. 34:19). Therefore, they think bodily diseases are sent by God and there is no use to resist them.

This kind of an argument will not stand up in view of all the other passages where the word "affliction" is found. It is found 177 times and only once is it clear that it refers to physical sickness (Ps. 107:17-20). Not even James 5:13 is clear that it refers to sickness, for sickness is not mentioned by James until verse 14. *Affliction* is used many ways other than in reference to sickness, such as: "man afflicting man" (Gen. 15:13; Ex. 1:11); "husbands afflicting wives" (Gen. 31:50); "men afflicting their own souls" (Lev. 16:29-31); "loss of loved ones" (Ruth 1:21); "family troubles" (Gen. 29:32); "imprisonment" (Ps. 107:10; Phil. 4:14); "persecutions" (1 Th. 1:6); "trials" (Isa. 48:10); "wars" (Ps. 44:2; Isa. 9:1); and "fastings" (Isa. 58:5). Men are also spoken of as afflicting themselves (Jas. 4:9; Lev. 16:29). Both God and Christ are spoken of as being afflicted (Isa. 53:4, 7; 63:9; Col. 1:24).

Shall we say that God the Father, Christ, and every person referred to in these Scriptures had bodily diseases when they were afflicted, or that all these kinds of afflictions are physical diseases? In this case none of these Scriptures would make sense. Yet in the Christian realm, the word "affliction" is almost always (but with few exceptions) used to refer to sickness. The Hebrew and Greek words for "affliction" mean "to look down," "browbeat," "depress," "abase self," "humble self," "displease," "hurt," "vex," "grieve," and "be sad." God never sends any of these trials. Sin and Satan are to blame for such afflictions as well as for sickness. Therefore, do not blame God for any ill that comes to anyone. If He is not the cause of these afflictions, then one can freely in faith ask Him for help in these sufferings, and He will fulfill His promise and deliver. If the sick one wants to insult God by laying the blame on Him and using this as an excuse for his unbelief, then let him stay sick. There is nothing God will do for him until he is awakened from his delusion and brought to faith and humility.

That Sickness is Sent by God

It is stated in Exodus 15:26; Leviticus 26:14-46; Numbers 14:12; Deuteronomy 28:20-68; 1 Chronicles 21:14; Job 33:14-29 and other passages that God sends and appoints sicknesses to men, but all such passages must be understood as being the permission of God when men failed Him and sinned. In no passage do we read that God sent and brought upon men—at least those who were truly saved and obedient to His whole will—any sickness or disease. Such statements are always in connection with rebels against Him, as can be seen in the passages cited above, and in many others. God definitely promises to keep His own people in health and free from disease, so those who claim to be the people of God can claim healing and health from God upon the authority of the promises of God and the atonement of Christ (Ex. 15:26; Ps. 91; Isa. 58; Mt. 7:7-11; 8:17; 21:22; Mk. 11:22-24; Jn. 14:12-15; 15:7, 16; 1 Pet. 2:24; 3 Jn. 2). If men who are Christians want to make God a liar and claim that they are in the will of God by remaining sick, then let them go without the benefits of the gospel.

When God is spoken of as sending sickness it is meant that He withdraws His power and restraining hand from satanic powers who are always ready to destroy men and cause them untold sufferings (Jn. 10:10; Acts 10:38). For example, it was Satan that brought upon Job all his sufferings (Job 1:6-12; 2:1-12; 42:10). When it is said that the Lord would send a plague on Israel, it is also clear that Satan caused it (1 Chr. 21:1-15). When it is said that God sent Joseph into Egypt we have to understand that God permitted it but that Ishmaelites actually did this together with his brothers (Ps. 105:17; Gen. 37). So it goes, Satan and demons are the direct agents of sickness and disease.. God only made the law of sowing and reaping and it must be executed by the proper agents.

It is definitely stated in Luke 13:16; Acts 10:38; John 10:10; 1 John 3:8 that sicknesses are the works of the devil, so we have to believe demons are the direct agents in making men sick. When men quit blaming God for their troubles and cooperate with Him against demons they will get healed. As long as they maintain that such works of the devil are works of God, then God cannot help them get delivered from demonic powers.

That Healing, Miracles, and All Inspiration Ceased 64 A. D.

One of the most insensible and foolish arguments of unbelief today is that divine healing, the gifts of the Spirit, miracles, and all supernatural inspiration and manifestations ceased in 64 A.D. or when the apostles died. In the first place, all the apostles did not die by 64 A.D. Second, there is not one passage that teaches such a theory. The Bible promises healing throughout this age, as we have seen. History has recorded multiplied thousands of healings by God in this age since the apostles died. We know of thousands today that have been healed and can produce them to testify in any court that they have been miraculously healed by God's power.

Those who claim miracles ceased in 64 A.D. use the case of Trophimus in 2 Timothy 4:20 to prove that the day of miracles was over and that Paul and others had lost their power by that time.

But this example does not prove this. The Greek word for "sick" here is *astheneo* from *asthenes*, meaning "feeble," "strengthless," and "weak." It does not always mean that sickness is from some disease. It is translated "without strength" (Rom. 5:6); "weak in faith" (Rom. 4: 19; 14:1-2); "weak" law (Rom. 8:3); "weak" conscience (1 Cor. 8:7-12); "weak" people (1 Cor. 9:22); "weak and beggarly elements of the world" (Gal. 4:9); and "weak" in boldness (2 Cor. 11:21, 29; 13:3). It is also used of humility and dependence upon God (2 Cor. 13:3, 4, 9). Not one time is physical sickness referred to in these passages.

Trophimus was no doubt run down in body and had a physical breakdown because of his many labors for Christ and he needed to stay at Miletum to regain strength and rest for a while. This is definitely stated of Epaphroditus who had a physical breakdown because of overwork, and who was brought back to health by proper rest and faith (Phil. 2:25-30). No doubt it is true that many people in the days of the Apostles did not exercise faith and get healed, as is stated of many Corinthians (1 Cor. 11:29-32), but that does not do away with God's plan and provision for all who will believe. Multitudes were not saved through the ministry of the Apostles and yet shall we say that salvation ceased when the apostles died? This would not be a logical conclusion and there-fore it would not be a good excuse for unbelief about healing.

Divine healing does not give us liberty to abuse our bodies and overwork ourselves. We need proper rest and care for the body if a breakdown is to be avoided, and rest is certainly necessary when one has such a break-down. Just because Trophimus had to stay at Miletum to regain bodily strength, this does not do away with the many promises that God will heal all who pray in faith. Even if his case was that of a disease, it does not set aside one promise any more than the case of Judas being lost sets aside the plan for salvation from sin. Such arguments come solely from unbelief in the whole Word of God and willful rebellion against truth, or, if not from these, it comes from willful ignorance of the Bible. If Paul, Peter, and every other biblical character had all known diseases all of their lives and died with-out receiving the benefits of the gospel, this would not prove that healing is not in the atonement and not for believers today. The Bible is true whether anyone ever gets saved from sin, healed of diseases, or receives even one of the benefits that it promises. Those who fail to get what God has promised are no examples to follow. Their failures do not disprove the Bible, instead, they prove their unbelief in God and in the Bible.

That All Men in the Bible Were Not Healed

Another common excuse made for unbelief is that not everyone in the Bible was healed, so everyone today cannot be healed. Of course, if someone tried to obtain healing today like King Asa did in 2 Chronicles 16:12-14, or Ahaziah in 2 Kings 1), or like the woman of Mark 5:24-26, he would likely fail to be healed. But if we take all the hundreds of examples in Scripture and follow the means of healing they used, we would certainly find the healing we seek. Not a single failure to receive healing is recorded where men and women met the conditions of God. There never will be a failure to receive divine healing where faith is exercised in God and the Gospel. As seen above in Point 5, failure on the part of any man in any age to receive what God promises only proves his unbelief. It does not do away with the provision made for him, nor does it make God a liar.

It is often said that even Jesus did not heal everybody, and Mark 6:5 is always given as proof, but nothing is said in this passage about Jesus failing to heal anyone for whome He prayed. It is clear here that He healed all who came to Him. The reason He did not heal all in the city was because they did not come to Him for healing. Anyone can be healed today if they will obey the gospel. Everyone can still find the healing they want and need, if only they will do what God requires—know the truth and believe it without wavering (Jas. 1:5-8; Heb. 11:6; Mk. 11:22-24; Jn. 15:7, 16).

That Human Remedies Were Provided in Scripture

Others excuse their unbelief by claiming human remedies were used in Bible days instead of spiritual and divine means to heal sicknesses. Hezekiah's poultice is used by some to prove God commanded human remedies, but a casual reading of Isaiah 38 will show that his life already was prolonged fifteen years before the poultice was applied. The poultice was used for cleansing only, for there is nothing curative about such a poultice of figs. If this were not so, men would be using this particular kind of poultice today to heal. In this case it was Isaiah who advised use of the poultice, not the Lord; God did the healing, not the poultice. If God had not added fifteen years to his life all the poultices in the world would not have helped him.

Some stumble over Timothy's stomach and excuse their unbelief. They live in sickness when they could be well, if they would only believe God. The admonition to Timothy in 1 Timothy 5:23 was dietetic only. A little grape juice would never cure any stomach. It is beneficial to drink a little grape juice instead of "water only." One would naturally have stomach trouble if he had to drink stagnant rain water that is gathered during the rainy seasons as was the case where Timothy was laboring for the Lord. One cannot believe the New Testament and think that Paul taught Timothy unbelief, or that God would not heal any more, for Paul was a great man in power with God (Acts 19:11-12; Rom. 15:18-19, 29).

All of Paul's power would not take away such advice to Timothy under the circumstances. The water of Asia Minor was bad at certain seasons of the year due to the lack of rain and much suffering was thus caused. This advice to Timothy must be understood in this light, but it should never be used to excuse unbelief in God or His promises. Thus, we must conclude that human remedies do not set aside God's power to heal, and they do not nullify the atonement in any degree.

That Paul Had a Thorn in the Flesh

Some people stumble over Paul's thorn in the flesh and claim that God will not heal some people. His thorn in the flesh was not weak or diseased eyes as most men teach. It was plainly "an angel of Satan," for the Greek word for "messenger" in 2 Corinthians 12:7 means "angel" and not a disease. This angel followed Paul and caused all the sufferings he listed in 2 Corinthians 11, which were sent to keep him humble lest he should be exalted above measure.

The expression "thorn in the flesh" should be understood in the same sense it is understood in Numbers 33:55; Joshua 23:13; Judges 2:3; 8:7. In these passages no disease is mentioned, for they refer to the wars and hardships Israel was going to go through at the hands of the giants they had refused to kill. The thorn in Paul's flesh, therefore, refers to the sufferings the angel of the devil caused him to endure, as proven in 2 Cor. 4:8-18; 6:1-10; 11:16-33; 12:7-11; 1 Cor. 4:9-17. The word "buffet," used in 2 Corinthians 12:7 of Paul, is never used of "sickness," as proven where it is used (Mt. 26:67; 1 Cor. 7:11; 1 Pet. 2:20). Therefore, whatever it was that was buffeting Paul to keep him humble had to be some supernatural person, in order for this passage to harmonize with the rest of Scripture.

The Scriptures used to prove Paul had a physical disease do not say anything about bodily sickness. The word "weak" in 1 Corinthians 2:3; 4:10 should be understood of *humility and dependence upon God,* as explained under Point 5, above. The passage in 2 Corinthians 10:10 states only what was reported about him, not that it was a true report. But if we are going to understand the word "weak" in this passage to prove he had a disease, then we should make the same word mean the same thing in 2 Corinthians 11:29 where he said "I am not weak" or "I am not sick." In that case, the argument concerning the other passage would be of no effect to prove he had a disease that made him weak. The words "affliction" and "chasten" in 2 Corinthians 6:4, 9 do not refer to disease any more than the same words do in other Scriptures, as explained already in Points 2 and 3, above.

The final passages we'll look at that are used to prove Paul had sore eyes are Galatians 4:15 and 6:11, but neither of these passages state that he had the common oriental eye disease called *ophthalmia*, which made him almost blind. The first of these two passages could best be understood as a figure of affection for Paul. Just like one might say today, "I would give my right eye for that," or "you would give your right limb for me, you love me so." We would not have to believe that the speaker had a right eye or a leg full of disease. These are mere figures of speech, expressing affection. Concerning Galatians 6:11, "Ye see how large a letter I have written with mine own hand." The Greek word for "letter" is *gramma*, meaning "a writing", "a letter," "note," "epistle," "book," "bill," or "document." Paul could not possibly have been so blind that he had to write big letters in his words, for if he were as blind as this, he could not have written an epistle at all. It would not have been readable if he had written it. Galatians was a long epistle, longer than seven of Paul's epistles and as long as two others. In some ancient manuscripts, Hebrews was attached to Galatians with this phrase,

"Pros Hebrios," meaning to the Hebrews, and if this be the case, these epistles together would make this writing of Paul longer than any of his other separate works. At any rate, we can disregard the "sore eye" theory, as there is nothing to support it in Scripture.

If men would seek half as hard for an excuse to believe God as they do for an excuse to disbelieve Him, they would receive more of the benefits of the gospel. One of the greatest regrets of Heaven will be that when we get there, and we see how fully God had provided for our needs on Earth and how anxious He was to bless us with the abundance of everything, we will wish we had believed Him more in this life. Let us now wake up to the greatness of His promises and refuse to let any man or demon rob us of the full benefits of the Gospel that are ours now.

Chapter Thirteen

BIBLICAL PROOF THAT IT IS ALWAYS GOD'S WILL TO HEAL

There are many reasons we can give from Scripture to prove that bodily healing is always the will of God for all men in every age. *The following proofs are a few that are backed by many Scriptures to prove it is always God's will to heal:*

(1) Healing is in the atonement and therefore must be the will of God for all men for whom the atonement was made. That healing is in the atonement is plainly stated in a number of Scriptures. The literal rendering of Isaiah 53:3-5 reads, "He was despised, and forsaken of men; a man of pains, and acquainted with sickness: . . . Surely he hath borne our sicknesses, and carried our pains: yet we did esteem him violently beaten, slain of God, and degraded. But he was slain for our crimes, he was beat to pieces for our guilt; . . . and with his wounds we are healed. . . Yet it pleased Jehovah to beat him to pieces; he hath made him sick: when thou shalt make his soul and offering for sin." This plainly pictures Christ as bearing the sins and sicknesses of all men in His own body on the cross.

To prove that Isaiah meant healing of the body instead of only forgiveness of sins we have the statement of Matthew 8:16-17 saying, "He cast out the spirits with his word, and healed all that were sick: that it might be fulfilled which was spoken by Isaiah the prophet, saying, Himself took our infirmities, and bare our sicknesses." Peter also taught that Christ took our sicknesses on the cross: "Who his own self bare our sins in his own body on the tree, that we, being dead to sins, should live unto righteousness: BY WHOSE STRIPES YE WERE HEALED" (1 Pet. 2:24). Paul taught the same truth when he stated that many of the Corinthians were sick and many had died because they had failed to get healing for the body by rightly discerning the Lord's broken body (1 Cor. 11:29-30).

To say that Matthew 8:17 was fulfilled before the atonement was made on the cross, and therefore, it was not fulfilled on the cross, does not prove that healing is not in the atonement. On the same basis we could prove that Christ did not atone for sin on the cross because He also forgave sins before the cross. But 1 Peter 2:24 settles this question by showing that both sins and sicknesses were atoned for by Christ in His sufferings. Also, since Isaiah 53 pictures Christ's sufferings on the cross, it proves that both sins and sicknesses were borne by Him at that time. Christ forgave sins and healed before the cross in view of His coming atonement for both.

(2) God would not have healed people in both Testaments if it had not been His will to heal all who came in faith to him. God is no respecter of persons (Rom. 2:11), and He has told us if anyone has a respect of persons he has sinned (Jas. 2:9). This proves that God will heal all alike if He has ever healed anyone. Everyone can be healed the same way that others have been healed and they have the same right to such healing

as all others have had, for it is God's promise to provide for all alike and be good to all alike (Ps. 84:11; Mt. 7:7-11). This is why Jesus died (Mt. 8:16-17; 1 Pet. 2:24; Rom. 8:32).

(3) God would not have made plain His will concerning healing, if it were not His will to always heal those who meet His conditions of healing (Mt. 8:17; Jas. 5:14-16; 1 Pet. 2:24; 3 Jn. 2).

(4) God would have been the originator of sin and sickness, if it had been His will for such to continue in the human race (Rev. 21:3-7).

(5) He would not have healed even one person in any age and He would not have provided for and freely promised healing at all if He were responsible for sickness (Jn. 10:10).

(6) It was God's will that man should be healthy and sinless forever when He created him, and that is still His highest will (Gen. 2:17; 3 Jn. 2).

(7) Jesus Christ proved it to be God's will to heal all the sick when He actually healed all that were oppressed of the devil (Acts 10:38).

(8) The universal will of God was made clear when the early church was given power to carry on the work Jesus "began both to do and to teach" (Acts 1:1-8; Mt. 29:19-20; Mk. 16:15-20; Jn. 14:12-15).

(9) The fact that sickness is the work of the devil proves that God wills to get rid of it in His children (1 Jn. 3:8; Jn. 10:10).

(10) Sin is also the will of God if sickness is, for both

were dealt with on the same basis (Mt. 9:1-12; Jas. 5: 14-16; Mt. 13:15).

(11) Satan and demons would not fight to make and keep men sick if it was the will of God for them to be sick. Satan would try to make men well if it was the will of God for them to be sick.

It is an unfailing principle of Satan to work just the opposite of the will of God. When one argues that it is God's will for them to be sick he is in cooperation with Satan and not God (Acts 10:38; 1 Jn. 3:8; Jn. 10:10).

(12) Jesus would not have died to heal men of sickness if it is the will of God for them to be sick, and if He wanted men to bear it (Mt. 8:16-17; Jn. 10:10; 14:12-15; Acts 10:38; 1 Pet. 2:24).

(13) Every time men asked Christ to heal He did it, repeatedly saying, "I will" (Mt. 8:2, 7; Jn. 5:60). Since He spoke only as God gave Him words, then He expressed the will of God in saying "I will" (Jn. 12: 49).

(14) There can be no analogy between Christ's prayer, "If it be thy will" and the prayers of Christians concerning God's will to heal. Healing is always of God and is always His will. We do not have to ask God His will concerning anything that is definitely promised in Scripture. It is already His will to heal or He would not have given His Word that it is. In other words, any promise God has made should never once be doubted, and asking God whether His promise is true expresses doubt and unbelief. The promises to the believer are "ask what ye will" and "What things soever ye desire," therefore ask, and you shall have them (Mk. 11:22-24;

Jn. 14:12-15; 15:7, 16; 16:23-26; Mt. 21:2122; Jas. 1:5-9; Heb. 11:6). How foolish it is to ask God to know His will concerning anything that is already clearly His will! Never be guilty again of praying a useless, unbelieving prayer concerning anything that God has promised, such as "If it be thy will." It is a sinful reflection upon God to always tell Him that you do not believe His will as expressed in plain promises.

(15) Sick people should ask God to forgive their unbelief even when they are only tempted to question the will of God concerning healing or any of His promises. The will of God is expressed in the Lord's prayer, "Thy will be done in Earth AS IT IS *IN* HEAVEN" (Mt. 6:10). If one could be presumptuous enough to argue that Heaven is full of sick people and that therefore, this must also be God's will on Earth, one might question the will of God and excuse unbelief. This prayer has been perverted by Christians almost universally. Even Christian hymns and writings disclose such delusions of Satan to keep men in bondage to himself. Christians actually thank God for the work of the devil. Satan also leads them to believe that his works in their bodies glorify God and that they are in His perfect will by having sicknesses. A clear sample of such fallacy is expressed in the following hymn of Frances Ridley Havergal, written in the Alps, Oct. 8, 1876, while she was in great pain:

> "I take this pain, Lord Jesus, from thine own hand; The strength to bear it bravely thou wilt command. I take this pain, Lord Jesus, as proof indeed that thou art watching closely my truest need, that thou, my Good Physician, art watching

still, that all thine own good pleasure thou wilt fulfill. I take this pain, Lord Jesus; what thou dost choose. The soul that really loves thee will not refuse. I take this pain, Lord Jesus, as thine own gift. And true, though tremulous praises I now up lift. 'Tis thy dear hand, O Saviour, that presseth sore. The pressure only tells me thou lovest me."

What wonderful love and what a way to express it! This is accusing Christ of being the author of pain and sickness for the pleasure of God; that sickness proves the love of God; that it is the truest need of man; that the Good Physician instead of healing, makes sick; that it is God's pleasure to cause pain in His children; and that such is the choice of God and His gift to the redeemed.

One can only believe that such poetry was inspired of Satan instead of God. And to think saints are so deceived! Surely Satan stands back and laughs with glee when he can get God's own children to accuse Him of putting on them the works of the devil.

(16) It is as impossible for God to communicate disease as it is for Him to communicate and propagate sin and rebellion. Neither sin nor sickness comes from God, for they do not belong to Him. They belong to a fallen world of sinful creatures (Jas. 3:11-12).

(17) It is not presumptuous to always pray for healing, believing from the whole heart that it is already God's will and that it shall be done according to His will (Jn. 10:10; 15:7; Jas. 4:7; 5:14-18; Mk. 11:22-24).

(18) If it were not the will of God to always heal, He never would have provided the means of healing, made a covenant to heal, promised healing, demonstrated it,

rebuked men for not having faith for it, and continued to heal in every age. He never would have made healing part of the spiritual equipment of the church and proof that an individual is a full believer (Jn. 14:12; 1 Cor. 12: 7-11; Acts 1:8; 3:6; 4:30; 5:10; 19:11; etc.)

When Should Men Pray "If It Be Thy Will"?

It is clear by now that it is sinful to pray, "If it be thy will" concerning any of God's promises. This kind of prayer is a prayer of unbelief, and it will never be answered. This type of prayer does not take God at His Word, nor does it believe that God means what He says. It calls God into question concerning the things He has assured men that they will receive—if they will only have faith. Thus one should never pray such prayers as: "If it be thy will, save this man and forgive him of his sins," "If it be thy will, heal this man and make him well," "If it be thy will, supply my needs and make me a success in business," or "If it be thy will, please give me what you have promised." In fact, this phrase, "If it be thy will" should never be used in ordinary praying for any good thing that God has promised.

The only time such a prayer should be made is when we make plans to "go to such and such a city, to buy and sell to get gain," or to do something that is not covered by the promises of God in His Word (Jas. 4: 13-17). In such matters it is proper to discover the will of God before acting, and never act until God's will is made clear. Never go to God as if you are afraid, and as if you expected Him to upbraid you. He does not do this (Jas. 1:4-8). Learn the will of God concerning your personal plans that are not mentioned in particular in any Scripture, as you read the Bible and pray, and then do the will of God. Do not pray to change God or to get Him to agree with your plans, but pray until you are changed and willing to conform to God's plan for you. In other words, learn what God has promised in His Word and never pray, "If it be thy will" concerning these facts. Pray to know the will of God concerning all other matters and all prayers can be prayed in faith and confidence as to the answer.

Chapter Fourteen

HOW TO GET HEALED AND STAY HEALED

Become Converted and Born Again

The gospel teaches that forgiveness of sin and healing of the body go hand in hand. If ministers would teach the entire gospel, people would have faith in both healing and forgiveness and sinners could get both at the time of conversion. The following Scriptures prove that both benefits were provided in the sacrifice of Calvary: "Himself took our infirmities, and bare our sicknesses" (Mt. 8:16-17); "Who his own self bare our sins in his own body on the tree, that we, being dead to sins, should live unto righteousness: by whose stripes ye were healed" (1 Pet. 2:24). The following passages prove that both forgiveness of sins and healing of the body should be received at one time: "Who forgiveth all thine iniquities; who healeth all thy diseases" (Ps. 103:3); "For whether is easier to say, Thy sins be forgiven thee; or to say, Arise, and walk?" (Mt. 9:5); "For this people's heart is waxed gross, and their ears are dull of hearing, and their eyes they have closed; lest at any time they should see with their eyes, and hear with their ears, and should understand with their heart, and should be converted, and I should heal them" (Mt. 13:15); "Is any sick among you? Let him call for the elders of the church; and let them pray over him, anointing him with oil in the name of the Lord: And the prayer of faith shall save the sick, and the Lord shall raise him up; and if he have committed sins, they shall be forgiven him" (Jas. 5:14-16). Thus, it is very clear that healing is just as easy to receive from God as forgiveness of sins. Both can be received by the same simple faith in God and asking in the name of Jesus. Healing is part of your salvation; do not be cheated out of it any more than you permit yourself to be cheated out of forgiveness of sins.

Once I was called at 6:00 a.m. to pray for a woman that had been having convulsions since three o'clock the previous afternoon. Her tongue was sticking out of her mouth like a beef steak. A large spoon had to be put between her teeth to keep her from chewing her tongue. She was having one convulsion after another, and the doctor had just left saying there was no hope and that he could do no more to help her. After I had spoken to the husband and others in the room about prayer and had told them that God was able to do what man had failed to do, and after the husband promised to serve God if his wife was healed, we all kneeled and had prayer. She was no better; so I said to the young man who had come along with me, "Let us go into the woodshed and pray until we know that God has answered prayer." There were some unbelievers in the home who were scoffing at healing through prayer, so we thought it best to get by ourselves and pray without any distraction. We prayed until about 10:30 a.m. and then went into the house and had one more prayer, having the assurance that God had already answered prayer. The woman turned over on her side and went to sleep and slept all afternoon The next day when we went to see her, she was perfectly well. I met this woman again in California just last year, and she testified to the fact that she had been healed in answer to prayer. God will do anything when conditions are met. If you have need of healing, it is only right that you surrender your life to God if you expect Him to heal you. You will not only get healed, but you will be saved at the same time—if you are not already saved from a life of sin.

Have Faith in God for Healing

If we will ask God for healing and believe that it is done, in exactly the same way that we are taught to ask for forgiveness of sins, it will be done. We should never doubt for one moment that God will heal us, just as we are taught to believe in the forgiveness of sins. We should resist all doubt that we are healed, just as we must if we are tempted to doubt that God has forgiven us. We are taught to accept salvation by faith and count it done whether we feel it or not. We are taught that God has forgiven us regardless of our feelings; and if we will but believe this, we are saved. So it is with healing of the body. After prayer has been completed and healing has been asked for, we should likewise count it done and believe it regardless of feelings, symptoms, or outward evidences to the contrary.

If we will maintain that we are healed just as much as we do that we are forgiven, God will confirm and manifest the healing just as He does forgiveness of sins. This fact cannot be overemphasized, as healing depends much on this firm stand that prayer has been heard and answered. If you want the benefits of the gospel, do what is required to get these benefits, and you will not fail to get them.

We cannot guarantee the benefits according to the gospel until you meet these conditions. Are the benefits worth the efforts in meeting the conditions? If they are, then do as you are instructed. If they are not worth the effort to believe God without wavering, then do not fret because you do not get what you want. You cannot expect God to be a respecter of persons and give you these benefits when you fail to do as He requires. He is not that kind of God, and He will not break His laws for anyone. He knows that every individual can, if he will, choose to meet the conditions of unwavering faith. Do not baby yourself any longer or complain that it is hard to believe. This very attitude is sinful, and you should ask God to forgive you for believing lies and Satan in preference to truth and God. As long as you cooperate with Satan and allow unbelief, you cannot cooperate with God and exercise true faith. One cannot serve two masters or have faith and unbelief in his life at the same time (Mt. 6:24; Jas. 1:4-8).

In Detroit, Michigan, about four years ago a deacon of a certain church took me to pray with a man that was paralyzed on one side and who had not walked for about eight months. I spoke to him about his faith; and his very first words, as I recall, were, "I believe in healing all right, but I cannot seem to have faith for my healing." I got up and walked over to his bed and said, "Don't you say that again. That is a lie. You can have faith and you must have faith if you expect to get healed." I then quoted Mark 11:22-24 and emphasized the truth of verse

24 this way, "Believe you have got it and you shall have it." I repeated that several times and got him to promise to believe that God would heal him and then prayed. While I was praying, the paralyzed man said, "If I have got it, what am I lying here for?" With that he jumped out of bed and shouted all over the place. I said, "Now you stay up until bedtime and then go to bed and get up in the morning perfectly well. Forget that you ever had paralysis."

Quit Praying "If It Be Thy Will"

As we have seen in Chapter Thirteen, it is God's will to heal, because He has definitely promised to heal all who come to Him in faith. Let this be settled once and forever and never again question God or make Him a liar by saying, "If it be thy will." Since He has promised healing, it is sinful and contrary to both His Word and His will to pray this way. One should go to God in absolute unwavering faith for those things that He has promised. He should never question the will of God at all concerning what He has promised. To do so is to make God a liar by letting Him know that we do not believe His promises, or we doubt what He has said and we do not believe that He means what He says. It is His will to give what He has promised or He would not have made His will known by the promises.

A lady wrote some time ago and gave the following testimony: "My husband had been in the insane hospital for a long time and was not improving. But when we began to pray like you said and not say, 'If it be thy will,' the work was done. Thank God my husband is healed and back home with a good mind. This is a real testimony for he was in an awful shape." God will answer anyone who will quit doubting His Word and His will, and who will pray in faith according to the promises.

Wholly Trust God in Sickness and Adversity

The Bible says, "Cursed be the man that trusteth in man, and maketh flesh his arm, and whose heart departeth from the Lord . . . he shall be like the heath in the desert . . . Blessed is the man that trusteth in the Lord, and whose hope the Lord is . . . he shall be as a tree planted by the waters . . . and shall not see when heat cometh, but her leaf shall be green [shall have health] . . . neither shall cease from yielding fruit" (Jer. 17:5-10. See also Pr. 3:5-8; 2 Chr. 16:12-14; 2 Ki. 1:1-17; Mk. 5:25-34).

Obey God and His Word

"My son, forget not my law; but let thine heart keep my commandments: for length of days, and long life, and peace, shall they add to thee" (Pr. 3:1-8); "Attend to my words; incline thine ear unto my sayings . . . for they are life unto those that find them, and health to all their flesh" (Pr. 2:1-5; 3:13-24; 4:20-23); "If ye abide in me, and my words abide in you, ye shall ask what ye will, and it shall be done unto you" (Jn. 15:7; 1 Jn. 3:21-22; 5:14-15. See also Ex. 15:26; Dt. 4:40; 7:12-15; 28:1-62; 30:1-20; Ps. 105:37; 107:20).

Make Peace with Fellow Men

"When ye stand praying, forgive, if ye have ought against any: that your Father also which is in heaven may forgive you your trespasses" (Mk. 11:22-26); "Confess your faults one to another, and pray one for another, that ye may be healed" (Jas. 5:14-16).

Call Church Elders and Believe in Their Prayers

"Is any sick among you? Let him call for the elders of the church; and let them pray over him, anointing him with oil in the name of the Lord: and the prayer of faith shall save the sick" (Jas. 5:14-16); "They shall lay hands on the sick, and they shall recover" (Mk. 16:17-20).

Many ministers today can testify of miraculous healings in the lives of people who have obeyed James and called for prayer. Multiplied thousands of people are being healed every day by obeying this divine prescription. In almost every church there are many witnesses to the power of God to heal the body by faith in the name of Jesus Christ.

About four years ago in Washington, Pennsylvania, I was called to the hospital to pray for a lay preacher by the name of John Miller. He had fallen forty–seven feet off the roof of a building he was working on. He was carried to the hospital, and the X–ray showed that his back was broken in two places and three vertebrae were fractured. I reached the hospital about 5:00 p.m. He was in such pain that large drops of perspiration were standing out on his forehead. Doctors told him that he would have to be in a cast for many months. I said to him, "Brother Miller, let us agree that God will hear and answer prayer and that He will heal you now. It matters not what doctors may say, what Christians will say, or what anyone will say to you. You will have men encourage your unbelief and tell you how long you will have to be in the hospital. Very few Christians will stand with you in faith that you will be instantly healed, but if you and I will agree in faith, you will be healed." I never will forget how he held my hand and in agony said, "I will agree with you."

We prayed and anointed him with oil, as James said, and the prayer of faith was prayed. God instantly removed all the pain, and he believed that he was healed. He told the doctors that he was healed. Another X–ray was taken, and it showed that there was no broken back and no vertebra was fractured. The doctors could not understand it. They had both X–rays. One showed a broken back and the other did not. A little soreness remained in his back a few days because of the great fall. Johnny Miller was up daily walking around and reading his Bible, testifying to everybody what God had done. He wanted to go home, but the doctors kept him in the hospital over two weeks under observation. They could not understand his case.

Two weeks and three days went by, and on this day Johnny was standing up in his room reading his Bible when the doctor came into the room. He asked if he could go home as he was feeling as fine as ever. The doctor said that if he would submit to a cast he could go home, as they would not be responsible for anything that would happen by letting him go home before it was safe. They could not yet figure out what had happened since they had the two X–rays showing two opposite things. He submitted to being put in a cast if they would release him. That night at home the Lord spoke to him and said, "Take your cast off, for I have healed you." He called up a friend in the city and told him to bring his tin snips and other tools over and help him get the cast off. The two of them worked for several hours, and when it was finally removed, Johnny jumped out of bed and went upstairs to the bathroom. Brother Miller was a living witness to the whole hospital staff and to many in the city that knew of his case.

Control the Tongue

"The mouth of a righteous man is a well of life . . . There is that speaketh like the piercings of a sword; but the tongue of the wise is health . . . He that keepeth his mouth keepeth his life; but he that openeth wide his lips shall have destruction . . . A wholesome tongue is a tree of life . . . pleasant words are as an honeycomb, sweet to the soul, and health to the bones . . . Death and life are in the power of the tongue" (Pr. 10:12; 12:18; 13:3; 15:4; 16:24; 18:21).

"What man is he that desireth life, and loveth many days, that he may see good. Keep thy tongue from evil, and thy lips from speaking guile" (Ps. 34:13-14; 1 Pet. 3:10-11; Jas. 3). It is interesting to note that nine of the eleven plagues upon Israel, as recorded in Numbers alone, were caused by the misuse of the tongue (Num. 11:1-3, 33-35; 12:1-16; 13: 26-33; 14:1-37; 16:1-50; 21:5).

Live in God and Under His Protection

"He that dwelleth [remains, settles down, or takes up a homestead] in the secret place of the Most High shall abide under the shadow [defense, protection] of the Almighty . . . I will say of the Lord, He is my refuge and my fortress: my God; in him will I trust. Surely he shall deliver thee from the snare of the fowler, and from the noisome pestilence. He shall cover thee with his feathers . . . his truth shall be thy shield and buckler. Thou shalt not be afraid for the terror by night; nor for the arrow that flieth by day; nor for the pestilence that walketh in darkness; nor for the destruction that wasteth at noonday. A thousand shall fall at thy side, and ten thousand at thy right hand; but it shall not come nigh thee . . . There shall no evil befall thee, neither shall any plague come nigh thy dwelling. For he shall give his angels charge over thee, to keep thee in all thy ways. They shall bear thee up in their hands, lest thou dash thy foot against a stone. Thou shalt tread upon the lion and adder; the young lion and the dragon shalt thou trample under feet . . . He shall call upon me, and I will answer him: I will be with him in trouble; I will deliver him and honour him. With long life will I satisfy him, and shew him my salvation" (Ps. 91).

To illustrate the power of the 91st Psalm I relate the following story. It is a true story that happened in my early ministry. About twenty–two years ago I was the principal of a Bible Institute in Dallas, Texas. One afternoon it was reported that two of the male students were sick in the men's dormitory. I gathered several students with me around the bed and prayed for the men, anointing them with oil as taught in James 5:14-16. One of the students was immediately healed and the other was not. It puzzled me for the moment that the same prayer and faith worked in one case and not in another.

This boy broke out with smallpox, and along with this a panic broke out in the school among the students. Most of them wanted to go home at once, as it was nearing the end of the school year and they did not want to be quarantined away from home for an indefinite period. The next morning in chapel we read the 91st Psalm and asked the students how many would agree together in faith that God would rebuke the plague and not permit anyone else to catch smallpox. I told them that since they were training for the ministry as pastors, evangelists, and missionaries, this test was good for them to prove the power of God in time of need.

Not one student raised his hand to say that he would agree with us. I was so surprised at this attitude that I wanted to know why they acted thus. Then they began to confess their faults to each other and ask for forgiveness for the little troubles that they had caused each other during the months of living in such close association with each other. After this was all over, I then asked how many would agree, and every hand went up. I then asked them to stand to their feet and praise God together for healing the boy who had the smallpox, and ask Him to stay the plague where it was.

Believe it or not, God did that very thing, and the other boy was healed instantly and the plague was stayed. Not one student who remained at school caught smallpox. Just one boy rebelled and refused to stay in school. He went home and caught smallpox.

Those who remained in school, where the protection of the blood of Christ and the power of God was claimed in faith, were kept free from the plague. We never did let the health officer of Dallas know about the plague. We fumigated the best we knew how and finished the school year in victory. This experience taught me that all things are possible to them that believe. Since then, on many an occasion, I have tested and proved the power of the promises of God and have always found them to be yea and amen to them that believe (2 Cor. 1:20).

Praise God in Faith for Healing

David said, "Bless the Lord, O my soul: and all that is within me . . . forget not all his benefits: who forgiveth all thine iniquities; who healeth all thy diseases" (Ps. 103:1-5). It is written of Abraham, "He staggered not at the promise of God through unbelief; but was strong in faith, giving glory to God; and being fully persuaded that, what he had promised, he was able also to perform. And therefore it was imputed to him for righteousness" (Rom. 4:17-22; Heb. 11:11-12). Paul said, "Be careful [anxious] for nothing; but in everything by prayer and supplication with thanksgiving let your requests be made known unto God" (Phil. 4:5-6; Heb. 13:15-16).

Serve God in Holiness as Earnestly as You Sought Him

"As ye have therefore received Christ Jesus the Lord, so walk ye in him; rooted and built up in him, and stablished in the faith, as ye have been taught, abounding therein with thanksgiving" (Col. 2:6-7); "sin no more, lest a worse thing come unto thee. . . Neither do I condemn thee: go, and sin no more" (Jn. 5:14; 8:11); "Beloved, if our heart condemn us not, then have we confidence toward God. And whatsoever we ask, we receive of him, because we keep his commandments, and do those things that are pleasing in his sight" (1 Jn. 3:21-22; 5:14-15). If one wants to keep his healing, let him keep his faith, live free from sin, and resist the devil who will try to bring back the sickness (Jas. 4:7; 1 Pet. 5:8-9).

Appropriate the Benefits of Calvary

Whosoever shall eat this bread, and drink this cup of the Lord, unworthily, shall be guilty of the body and blood of the Lord . . . For he that eateth and drinketh unworthily, eateth and drinketh damnation to himself, not discerning [comprehending the benefits by faith of] the Lord's body. For this cause many are weak and sickly among you, and many sleep" (1 Cor. 11:27-30); "What things soever ye desire, when ye pray, believe that ye receive them, and ye shall have them" (Mk. 11:24).

Resist the Devil—Refuse to be Denied

"Resist the devil, and he will flee from you. Draw nigh to God and he will draw nigh to you" (Jas. 4:7-8); ". . . the devil, as a roaring lion, walketh about, seeking whom he may devour: Whom resist steadfast in the faith" (1 Pet. 5:5-10. See also Eph. 6:10-18; 2 Cor. 10:4-7). How to resist will be fully explained in Chapter Sixteen, Points 11-14.

The following testimony illustrates what resistance to the devil can do for one. Mrs. R. M. G. of Georgia writes, "I was so weak I couldn't do my work and I had been that way for ten years. I was a total wreck. A Christian? Yes, but what I didn't know was that the devil was doing all that. I thought it was the Lord whipping me for something that I had done. But that day I turned it all over to God. I told Him that I meant to resist the devil from that day on and strength came into my body and I got up and went to work. I fully believe that God wants His children to be well in body."

Observe the Laws of God and of Nature

The body is God's house as well as our own. It belongs to God and not to us; "Know ye not that your body is the temple of the Holy Ghost which is in you, which ye have of God, and ye are not your own? For ye are bought with a price: therefore, glorify God in your body, and in your spirit, which are God's" (1 Cor. 6:19-20). As it is God's house, we are forbidden to mar it, to defile it, or to abuse it (1 Cor. 3:16-17; 6:19-20).

Common sense tells us that God can receive more glory from a body that is well and strong, because a person with such a body has complete use of all his faculties. A rugged constitution, a keen, alert mind, and unimpaired moral and spiritual faculties are necessary if one is to fully glorify God in the body and spirit. We can glorify God best by bearing much fruit (Jn. 15:8). To bear much and good fruit the tree or vine must be healthy and normally free from disease and things that cause fruit to become faulty (Mt. 3:10; 7:16-20). So it is with a Christian.

If God can receive glory from lives that are hindered by physical handicaps, how much more glory could He receive from the same people if they did not have such handicaps? Naturally, anyone with a physical handicap can do something, but they could do much more without any physical limitations.

Every person who wants health should see to it that he gets the proper food and eats it in the right way and in proper amounts from day to day. He should wear warm clothes and not expose his body to cold for the sake of style or fashion. He should take plenty of exercise and live in the open as much as possible. He should sleep in well–ventilated rooms with plenty of fresh air. He should see to it that the home gets plenty of fresh air through the day and each room gets as much sunlight as possible. He should have clean habits, bathe often, and keep his teeth in good shape. He should not overwork or abuse any part of his body. He should take plenty of rest and keep free from worry and anxiety. He should do everything possible to care for his body, soul, and spirit, according to the best knowledge he has, and he can have long life and happiness.

To be healthy one must control the mind and thoughts. Unclean thinking, reading of novels and love stories filled with immoral suggestions, admiring obscene pictures, obscene dancing, kissing, caressing, teasing, fondling, spooning, secret sins, dissipation, drinking, smoking, hatred, anger, worry, wrong eating, little sleep, overwork, lack of exercise, laziness, and other bad habits weaken the will and undermine our physical, mental, and moral health. Just good old–fashioned wholesome living will create life and energy, vitalize the blood, give elasticity and strength to the muscles, and build up physical health, bodily strength, and personal magnetism, beauty, and charm.

What the World Does to Maintain Health

All governments and organizations require physical fitness. They have certain standards of fitness for their employees and make provision that it be kept up to the highest peak of efficiency. They demand that the smallest accident or sickness be reported and every sore, illness, cold, etc., be taken care of at once in order to check the spread of the trouble to others. In every factory and public place we read signs such as "Be careful," "Watch that cold," "Don't expose your body," "Take exercise," etc. Many firms provide their employees certain places for recreation and exercise on their own time. We have laws that require physical fitness for marriage and for many public positions. Free clinics, medicine, advice, etc., are provided for those who cannot afford what they need to preserve their health.

Parents will spend their all and sacrifice everything in life to see that their children have the best of physical care and protection. They would heal their own children in a second if possible. Practically every human being would make some sacrifice to see their fellow men healed and enjoy good health. Men can fight and hate each other, but when sickness or death comes, the same men would aid their enemies to get well or have a decent burial if they die. Even most animals take care of their own and work to prolong the life and welfare of their own.

Does God Care and Make Provision for Health?

Is God the only Being in the universe that loves to see His own children, His own creation, His own workers, and those whom He professes to love to be sickly, puny, tired, worn, and good–for–nothing physically? Is He the only one who loves to see pain and disease in His own creation? Is He the only one who has not provided for the physical welfare of His own? Is He the only one who gloats over the handicaps of His children and desires them to be diseased so that He can be best glorified by seeing them sick? Is He the only one who prefers sickness to health; who would not heal His children when they get sick; who chastens His children by causing their lungs to be eaten up by disease, their limbs to rot off, their lives to linger between life and death in the most intense inhuman suffering for years upon years, and their lives to be destroyed by the enemies of both God and man; who would make a creation only to let it end in suffering and defeat and to die prematurely as manifest on every hand; and who wills these sin–cursed, disease–destroying agencies to take their toll of life and to cut off men before they finish their life work? Is He the only one who does not demand a high standard of physical fitness and efficiency among His workers? Is He the only one whose highest will is manifest by the sufferings, sicknesses, and helpless conditions of His people? Is He the only one who can get the best glory out of people when they are physically, morally, and spiritually deprived of their normal creative functions? Away with such slanderous concepts of God! He is not this kind of Being.

The Bible makes it clear that it is God's highest will for all men to "prosper and be in health, even as thy soul prospereth" (3 Jn. 2). The blame for wrong concepts of God is entirely upon man and the enemies of both God and man. Instead of meeting the conditions of the gospel to receive healing and stay healed, man continues to break the laws of God and nature—living in unbelief and rejection of God's way of healing and health in Christ. The sensible thing to do is to learn the cause of the trouble and remove it. Then one can be healed and stay healed.

Chapter Fifteen

Freedom from Poverty and Want

The idea that it is the will of God for man to suffer poverty; to be helpless, defeated, crushed, and sorrowful; to suffer pain, sickness, and disease—living from hand to mouth in order to keep himself humble and godly—is disproved by many plain Scriptures. Just the opposite is true, as we would naturally expect from the real, loving, kind, good and infinite Heavenly Father revealed in Scripture. We have no grounds for thinking of God as being such a brute, such an inhuman and ungodly despot and tyrant, as many teach that He is. There is not one in a thousand but what would say that God loves His own blood–bought spiritual sons and daughters much more than men love their own children. But there is hardly one in a thousand that is clear enough in their understanding of God to carry out this idea in their doctrines of God and His dealings with men. The following studies give the truth of the Bible on material prosperity:

The Definition of Providence

The word *providence* means "foresight" and "forethought," "the care of God over His creatures," "divine superintendence or direction for and over His creation."

Foresight and forethought on the part of anybody imply a future end, a goal, and a definite plan in attaining that end. All rational beings act with forethought and foresight; therefore, providence is an attribute all such beings have by nature. All rational beings and all animals exercise care and make provision for their own offspring. How much more is it true of the infinite God to make provision for and exercise infinite care over all His creation.

God's Care for Man is Infinite

Although all rational beings exercise providence according to their powers, the word reaches its full significance only when it is applied to the infinite God. The providence of God is the care and government He exercises over all things He has created in order that they may accomplish the ends for which they were created. It is the infinite care God takes of His universe, from the numbering of each hair of each head and the falling of each sparrow to the unfailing upholding of all things in the vast universe by His own power. It is the inherent nature of God which He exerts without intermission over all the works of His hands. It is the continual creation of God manifested in visible actions in the preservation and government of all things. It is that eternal power which is at work precluding all fortune, luck, and fortuitous accidents.

God's Care Particular for Converted Men

Providence may be considered as universal in reference to all things; special in reference to moral beings; and particular in reference to converted beings. Providence is the most comprehensive word in the language of theology. It is the background and the foundation of various doctrines of divine truth. It penetrates and fills the whole realm of relations between the creation and the Creator. It connects the unseen with the seen, the visible with the invisible, the creation with redemption, and personal salvation with the end of all things.

God Works for the Good of Creation

Providence, therefore, is that agency of God through Christ by the power of the Holy Spirit, by which through holy angels, redeemed men, and even demons and unsaved men, He makes all things work together for good to them that love the Lord and by which He makes all events of the physical and moral universe fulfill the original purpose for which it was created.

As creation explains the existence of the universe, and as preservation explains the continuance of the universe forever, so providence explains the working out of the purpose of God in all things according to the eternal purpose. It is a positive agency in the working out of all past and future events to the desired end of God. Providence is the actual control and care of God in the working out of His eternal plan. Since God's plan is all–comprehensive, the providence of God must also be all–comprehensive, embracing within it all the details, small or great, of the events of life and working to the ultimate purpose of God in all things.

Providence and Wealth

The Bible declares that God "giveth power to get wealth" (Dt. 8:17-18). When Solomon asked God for wisdom instead of wealth so that he would better be able to judge Israel, God gave him both. Solomon was one of the richest men that ever has lived, just because of the blessing of God. In fact, he was the world's first recorded billionaire. God also blessed Abraham, Isaac, Jacob, David, Job, and many men of the past with great wealth (Gen. 13:5-7; 24:1-35; 25:5; 26:12-16; 31:1-13; Job 42:10-17; 1 Chr. 22). It is in the power of God to make rich or to make poor (1 Sam. 2:7; Pr. 10:22; 1 Chr. 29:12).

Riches a Curse if Misused

If riches come to some men because of the blessing of God, then it is not a sin to have wealth. We are warned in Scripture not to misuse wealth to oppress the poor and not to permit riches to ensnare us into sin so that we forget God (Pr. 11:28; Mt. 13:22; Lk. 8:14; 1 Tim. 6:17; Jas. 5:1-6). There are a number of blessings the Bible lists as being better than riches, such as "righteousness" (Ps. 37:17); "a good name" (Pr. 22:10); and "life" (Pr. 14:24; 6:25-34). There are many other assets in life better than money; so one should not set his heart upon this as the chief objective in life. People with riches will have greater temptations, and often they will commit acts that they would not do if they did not have money. Riches are only temporary and should be recognized as such (Pr. 23:5; 27:24). Men are told not to set their hearts upon riches or trust in them, but to trust in the

Living God (Ps. 52:7; 62:10; 23:4; 1 Tim. 6:17). Many other statements are found in Scripture revealing the sins of the rich—how they oppress the poor, are boastful, proud, sinful, mean, and ungodly, because they have wealth and influence.

Riches a Blessing if Used Right

On the other hand, the Bible speaks of the many blessings of wealth when it is used in the right way—for the good of men and the glory of God. Wealth is a protection (Pr. 10:15; 18:11). It makes many friends (Pr. 14: 20). It makes one powerful (Pr. 22:7). It enables one to be rich in good works, and this in turn, if done in the right spirit (not to be seen of men, but because it is right to do good) will result in increased rewards in eternity (1 Tim. 6:18). Money is power in modern times, and every child of God could do infinitely more for God and lost souls if he had more of this kind of power. Think what could be done with riches in spreading truth and blessing men! There is no end to the good that one could do if he only had the means to do it.

Seeking Wealth Not a Sin

Looking at wealth from this standpoint, even praying to God for financial increase—and expecting it from Him in order to do more for the cause of God—is not a sin. Many people, even many Christians, sincerely doubt that God has a desire to see His children enjoying prosperity. Satan (and many church workers) warn believers against desiring wealth until it is an almost universal belief among Christians that wealth is more or less a sin. And yet, there is often a great deal of hypocrisy evident in our churces. Many doubt that God wishes to bless us financially, yet if a rich man becomes interested in a local church, or if he becomes generous in helping the work of Christ, he is greatly honored and respected. This honor should not be given him if it is a sin to have wealth, or to ask God for it. Such a man should never be recognized and his money should not be accepted, if indeed having wealth is a sin.

Anyone with a little bit of common sense knows there is nothing wrong in having wealth or in obtaining it in a rightful way. In fact, every child of God has many needs which he could and would have supplied if he had the money. As Christians, we often long to have more wealth in order to better support his family, his church, and the work of God in general. He does not consider this desire sinful, and if wealth would suddenly come to him he would still consider that he could be a true Christian if he used it rightly. Therefore, we have to conclude that the idea that it is wrong to pray for financial help is not only unscriptural, it is also unreasonable.

Unbelief, Not Wealth, is the Great Sin of Christians

The argument is often advanced at this point that it is not wrong to have wealth, but that there are many more important blessings for which we need to ask God. This is, after all, a mere excuse for unbelief. Men simply do not want to crucify their old traditions and theories and their unbelief and pray and ask God for financial help as they ask Him for physical or spiritual help. If we will learn the truth and ask God in faith, nothing will be financially impossible any more than physically or spiritually. Let us then be sensible and study the Bible from the standpoint of obtaining financial aid.

In the first place, let us ask ourselves the questions about this subject that we are beginning to ask concerning other things. Are we children of God? Does God really love us as we love our children? Would we will and desire our children to prosper? Does God will and desire anything less for His children than we do for our own? Why should He be different from man in desiring the best things in life for His children? What would there be sinful about God blessing His children with wealth? Jesus taught men the infinite Fatherhood of God, so naturally it would be His highest will for His children to be blessed with prosperity (Mt. 7:7-11; 3 Jn. 2).

God's Creative Purpose was that Men Should Prosper

God created man that he might be prosperous, healthy, successful, happy, wise, and blessed with all the good things that he could wish for in this life. He created all things and gave them all to man to use for his own good and pleasure. We see God's plan clearly in the opening chapters of Genesis,

> And God said, Let us make man in our image, after our likeness: and let them have dominion over the fish of the sea, and over the fowl of the air, and over the

cattle, and over all the earth, and over every creeping thing that creepeth upon the earth. So God created man in his own image, in the image of God created he him; male and female created he them. And God blessed them, and God said unto them, Be fruitful, and multiply, and replenish the earth, and subdue it: and have dominion over the fish of the sea, and over the fowl of the air, and over every living thing that moveth upon the earth.

Genesis 1:26-28, KJV

If it were sinful for us to have these things, God would not have given them to us to enjoy. The sin of man was not in being prosperous, healthy, and happy, but in eating the forbidden fruit. The world of abundance in which we live, here and now, proves that God wants man to have an abundance of every good thing in this life. God made enough for all and all can have everything they want, if only they will follow certain laws in order to obtain what they need.

Prosperity Need Not Cause Backsliding

The people that backslide when prosperous, healthy, and happy would backslide anyway; so if a few backslide when God blesses them with prosperity, let us not lose faith in the abundant love and providence of God. We must all learn to live Christian lives under all the conditions of life. Some people backslide over food, clothing, and other things that we all must have. Shall we quit eating? Shall we go naked? Shall we quit doing every good thing over which some stumble? Shall we conclude that such things are not the will of God because a few people backslide? Then do not argue this way about prosperity, health, and the abundant blessings of life that God wants all His children to enjoy. Stay saved and wisely use prosperity to help others, and God will bless you in greater abundance.

Scriptural Proof that God Wills Prosperity

God has definitely made many promises concerning the prosperity and happiness of His children. "Be thou strong and very courageous, that thou mayest observe to do according to all the law . . . turn not from it to the right hand or to the left, *that thou mayest prosper whithersoever thou goest* . . . thou shalt meditate therein day and night, that thou mayest observe to do all that is written therein: *for then thou shalt make thy way prosperous, and then thou shalt have good success*" (Josh. 1:5-9); "The Lord maketh poor, and *maketh rich*: he bringeth low, and lifteth up. He raiseth up the poor out of the dust, and lifteth up the beggar from the dunghill, to set them among princes, and to make them inherit the throne of glory" (1 Sam. 2:7-8); "And keep the charge of the Lord thy God, to walk in his ways . . . *that thou mayest prosper in all that thou doest, and whithersoever thou turnest thyself*" (1 Ki. 2:3-4); "Both *riches and honour* come of thee, and thou reignest over all; and in thine hand is *power and might*: and in thine hand it is *to make great, and to give strength to all*" (1 Chr. 29:12); "The hand of our God is upon all them *for good that seek him*: but his power and his wrath *is against them that forsake him*" (Ezra 8:22); "If they obey and serve him, they shall spend their days *in prosperity*, and their years *in pleasures*" (Job 36:11); "Blessed is the man that walketh not in the counsel of the ungodly nor standeth in the way of sinners, nor sitteth in the seat of the scornful. But his delight is in the law of the Lord; and in his law doth he meditate day and night. And he shall be like a tree planted by the rivers of water, that bringeth forth his fruit in his season; his leaf also shall -not wither; and *whatsoever he doeth shall prosper*" (Ps. 1:1-3).

The Psalm that is quoted by all Christians starts out with: "The Lord is my shepherd *I shall not want*" (Ps. 23:1). Other psalms give other promises such as: "They that seek the Lord *shall not want any good thing*" (Ps. 34:10); "Blessed be the Lord, who *daily loadeth us with benefits*" (Ps. 68:19); "*no good thing will he withhold from them that walk uprightly*" (Ps. 84:11); "Bless the Lord, O my soul, and *forget not all his benefits*: who *forgiveth* all thine iniquities; who *healeth* all thy diseases; who *redeemeth* thy life from destruction; who *crowneth* thee with loving kindness and tender mercies; who *satisfieth* thy mouth with good things; so that thy youth IS *renewed* like the eagle's" (Ps. 103:1-5).

God promised Israel abundant prosperity if she would conform to His will (Lev. 25:21; 26:4-9; Dt. 7:13-15; 15:4-6; 28:7-8). For Israel, as well as for God's people today, prosperity was to be a natural result of obedience to God and His Word.

In Deuteronomy alone, according to the Fenton translation of the Bible, the word "prosper" is used many times in place of "well with thee," as it is translated in the King James Version (Dt. 5:16, 29, 33; 6:3, 18; 12:28; 19:13). In Deuteronomy 30:15 this translation reads, "I put before you today life, and prosperity, and sin, and death." Thus prosperity is promised if men will quit the sin business. Although it is true that sinners sometimes prosper, they generally obtain their wealth through wrong dealings with their fellow men. The ungodly, however, will receive judgment for their sins, as we see clearly illustrated in Psalm 73, (Ps. 73).

Those who teach that Christians should be poor, sickly, and suffering all their days would naturally argue that these passages are in the Old Testament and refer to those living under the law of Moses. However, we reply that we are under a better covenant and have greater and better promises in the New Testament; so if these things were promised under the Old Covenant, they are for us in a greater way under the New Covenant. In 2 Corinthians 3:6-15 Paul argues that the glory and blessings of the Old Covenant were not as great as those under the New Covenant; so if men could obtain prosperity under the old, then it is certain they can get it under the New Covenant. In Hebrews, Paul argues that the New Covenant is a "better testament . . . established upon better promises" (Heb. 7:22; 8:6) and that the law was a "shadow of good things to come" (Heb. 10:1); so if a mere shadow produced prosperity, how much more will the realities of the New Covenant do the same?

Apart from this argument there are plain promises in the New Testament concerning prosperity: "What things soever ye desire, when ye pray, believe that ye receive them and ye shall have them" (Mk. 11:22-24); Ask and it shall be given you . . . for every one that asketh receiveth . . . If ye then, being evil, know how to give good gifts to your children; how much more shall your Father, which is in heaven, give good things to them that ask him? (Mt. 7:7-11); "For after all these things [good things of life] do the Gentiles seek; for your heavenly Father knoweth that ye have need of all these things. But seek ye first the kingdom of God, and his righteousness; and all these things shall be added unto you" (Mt. 6:31-33); "He that soweth sparingly shall reap also sparingly; and he which soweth bountifully shall reap also bountifully . . . God is able to make all grace abound toward you; that ye, always having all sufficiency in all things, may abound to every good work" (2 Cor. 9:6-8); "But my God shall supply all your need according to his riches in glory by Christ Jesus" (Phil. 4:19); "If ye abide in me, and my words abide in you, ye shall ask what ye will, and it shall be done unto you" (Jn. 15:7, 16); "Beloved, I wish above all things that thou mayest prosper and be in health, even as thy soul prospereth" (3 Jn. 2).

What could be more clear? How could God express His highest will any other way? Why should we limit God and His bountifulness to us just because we fear we may back-slide? Why not make up our minds that we will watch out for the dangers of riches and prosperity and act sensibly with what God blesses us? Why not use the blessings of God for His glory and the good of others?

God Promises All of Our Wants

God has promised to provide not only for all of our needs, but for all of our *wants as well*, provided they are not a desire for sin. All wants and needs are provided by God in the promises of the Gospel through Christ. The coomon idea among Christians today is that only our bare needs will be met by God—and that even these necessities are hard to obtain—but the Bible teaches that *all* wants of children of God are abundantly provided for, and that such supplies are easy for them to receive by faith: "All things are possible to him that believeth" (Mk. 9:23); "Have faith in God. For verily I say unto you, that *whosoever* shall say unto this mountain, Be thou removed, and be thou cast into the sea; and shall not *doubt in his heart: but shall believe* that those things which he saith shall come to pass; *he shall have whatsoever he saith.* Therefore I say unto you, *what things soever ye desire,* when ye pray, *believe that ye receive them,* and *ye shall have them*" (Mk. 11:22-24); "Verily, verily, I say unto you, He that believeth on me, the works that I do *shall he do also*; and greater works than these *shall he do*; because I go unto my Father, and *whatsover ye shall ask* in my name, *that will I do*, that the Father may be glorified in the Son. If ye shall ask *anything* in my name, *I will do it* . . . If ye abide in me, and my words abide in you, ye shall ask *what ye will*, and *it shall be done unto you* . . . I have chosen you and ordained you . . . *that whatsoever ye* shall ask of the father in my name, *he may give it to you* (Jn. 14:12-15; 15:7, 16; 16:23-26); "*whatsoever* we ask, we receive of him" (1 Jn. 3:21-22; 5:14-15).

These passages are so clear in themselves that they need no interpretation. All that is needed is faith in God and in His Word. If we believe the Bible, then it is settled that we believe that we can get whatever we ask in the name of Jesus. If we do not believe it, there is no need to try to get anything that we ask. That is how simple the whole program is. If we ask and believe, we receive. If we ask and do not believe, or if we do not ask because we do not believe, we do not receive.

God's plan for the needs of man becomes very clear when we accept at full face value the many simple promises of Scripture. There are no limitations in the provision made. The only limitations we find are those that come from man's unbelief and not from the plan itself. Because there are no limitations in the plan of God to get what we *want* as well as what we *need*, and because God gives "to all men liberally, and upbraideth not," let us have faith, nothing wavering, as required in James 1:5-8; Hebrews 11:6; Mark 11:22-24, and get what we want.

The doctrine that God's people should want for nothing is also taught in the Old Testament. David said, "The Lord is my shepherd, *I shall not want*" (Ps. 23:1-6). Again he said, "O fear the Lord, ye saints: for *there is no want* to them that fear him . . . they that seek the Lord *shall not want any good thing* . . . Delight thyself in the Lord: and He shall give thee *the desires of thine heart*" (Ps. 34:9-10; 37:3-6). Again we are told, "*no good thing* will He withhold from him that walketh uprightly" (Ps. 84:11).

Prosperity Needed in the Modern Church

Prosperity is needed by modern Christians in order to support missionaries, to help the work of God in the homeland, and to help the poor to be happy and healthy. If all Christians will appropriate the benefits of the promises as they should, all the financial problems of every local church and of the worldwide work for God will be taken care of. When Israel obeyed the Lord and brought their tithes and offerings to God, there were heaps upon heaps of supplies for God's work (2 Chr.

31:1-21). If all Christians were prosperous, there would be no need for the modern methods churches use to raise money. Some churches beg, gamble, and particpate in many unchristlike activities to keep the local work going. If all Christians were prosperous, minister would only have to make an appeal or merely give the people an opportunity to render to the Lord some of the abundance with which He has blessed them.

The Bible Program Will Bring Prosperity

If ministers will start a new program of teaching their people the Word of God and together with the people, believe the promises of God, and all pray for all the needs of the group, whether physical, financial, or spiritual, God Himself will demonstrate signs and wonders in meeting every need according to the faith exercised. They should make a Christian experiment along this line and see what God will do. God is meeting men who are following this program, and He will meet all His children if they will learn the truth and practice it.

To those who will honor God with their tithes and offerings, not because they want blessings, but because it is right to do it, God has promised, *"I will open to you the windows of heaven, and pour out a blessing, that there shall not be room enough to receive it"* (Mal. 3:9-11). If one argues that this was for Israel only we answer, it is also for the church according to Matthew 6:26-33; 10:29; Luke 6:38; 2 Corinthians 9:6-12; Philemon 4:19; 3 John 2. This last passage expresses the will of God for Christians: "Beloved, I wish *above all things that thou mayest prosper and be in health,* even as thy soul prospereth." Tithing is also taught in the New Testament (Mt. 23:23; Rom. 2:22; 1 Cor. 9:7-18; Heb. 7:1-11). Committing sacrilege in Romans 2:22 means to rob temples or to use God's money and consecrated things for himself.

God Works According to a Revealed Plan

A father in his family is the sovereign and does as he pleases within certain limits. God also acts within definite limits. He made man a free moral agent. As a matter of power God *might* predetermine certain volitions that would necessitate certain acts of man, but then *He* would be forcing men to act like a mere machine without freedom of action of his own accord. The question is therefore not what God *can* do, but what God *does* do in carrying out His own plan—a plan which was made to deal with free moral agents instead of machines. Therefore, we see that God must of necessity limit Himself in His actions in dealing with free moral agents and finite creatures.

God Recognizes Man's Free Moral Agency

Scripture, reason, and experience unite in teaching that man is morally free, that he is a free agent, and that he is not a mere machine to be acted upon by some other free moral agent. God's providential government is based upon the fact that He has to deal with free wills and rational beings like Himself. It consists in an intelligent revelation to man of his free moral agency and also of an administration by God in the affairs of men that would discourage sin and encourage holiness and conformity to the best state of being. God's providence must work upon two kinds of wills: those who are willing and those who are rebellious.

Willing Submission Does Not Destroy Free Agency

The child of God willingly submits to the whole will of God and receives many special and particular manifestations of providence. This does not destroy his free moral agency in any sense. It merely gives him the super–guidance that the fallen race should have. This kind of a will has divinely produced thoughts and feelings, hence divinely produced volitions. When such a free will chooses God and commits the ordering of his life to Him and prays and seeks for God to choose for Him what is best, that act in itself involves the highest form and the very essence of moral freedom and moral agency.

In the human realm, a perplexed child does not lose free agency when he asks a wise and all–loving father to decide a matter for him and to guide him in attaining a certain end. God will not, under the divinely appointed laws of moral government and free moral agency on the part of His creatures, work in and through the sinner and the moral rebel "to will and to do of his good pleasure" (Phil. 2:13; 2 Tim. 2:21). The sinner's will is bent on evil and opposed to the divine will. God's will does not work with, but against a sinful, rebellious will. If this working of God against the sinful will of man would determine its volitions, that would destroy free moral agency. God's providence then works only effectually through willing wills.

Providence even works with men who are not entirely subject to God, for there are different degrees of opposition. Many testify of the acts of providence before the will is fully surrendered. Much of the training in "chosen vessels" was brought about by unconscious preparation. The Holy Spirit seeks every possible way to guide man to a higher plane of life and to a life that is prepared and planned by God for him:

> Or despisest thou the riches of his goodness and forbearance and longsuffering; not knowing that the goodness of God leadeth thee to repentance?
> *Romans 2:4, KJV*

The free will of man is the only barrier that will ever stand in the way of his best interests. Divine providence, then, is limited and conditioned by a sinful free will. The only way God could prevent free moral agents from sin, accidents, rebellions, and other free acts of the will is by not creating them. For God to place one free will under irresistible divine restraint and compulsion would destroy free moral agency. If this were done, then not only all sin, but all virtue and holiness as attributes of the free will would be destroyed, for only such beings as can put forth free and holy volitions can put forth sinful volitions. The sinful and fallen race needs providence to guide it back to God and develop holy character and the highest moral service for the good of being and of the universe.

Evil to Saints Permitted, Not Caused by God

Many happenings that befall God's children occur through the sins of others, the rebellion of men against God, the conditions caused by reaping what is sown, or by some demonic power causing them to act contrary to the will of God. That good men suffer at the hands of evil men is a well–known fact. That Satan causes many of God's people to suffer is also well–known. God may or may not prevent certain disasters that befall His people. His decision depends upon the time, place, and conditions of the times in which the people live. Sometimes this is the only way God can work out His plan in certain individuals or classes of people.

Sometimes God has overruled the workings of evil men against His children so that they were not destroyed. This was true of Joseph, Moses, David, Daniel, Paul, Peter, and others. On the other hand, God has permitted certain ones to be destroyed. This is true of Abel, Jehu, Stephen, James, and others. The child of God must say with Paul if ever he is faced with like circumstances, "Christ shall be magnified in my body, whether it be by life, or by death." It was necessary that Christ should die for the sins of the world. Such was necessary in the working out of the divine plan. In the war on saints as in the early church or in certain other periods of time, the cause of God was advanced much faster and the power of God was made more manifest by such war than if things had gone smoothly for the cause of God. Jesus taught that "except a grain of wheat fall into the ground and die it abideth alone, but if it dies it bringeth forth much fruit" (Jn. 12:24). Again, "the blood of the martyrs is the seed of the church" has been a true saying in many periods of history.

Purpose and Final End of Providence

The purpose and final end of providence is to get all men to see their own need of guidance and care from an all–wise, infinite, Heavenly Father, and to consecrate themselves to the same end to which God is consecrated—the highest good of being and of the universe. It is by God's longsuffering and His patience, mercy, and goodness to stubborn rebels that many free moral agents are becoming broken and willing to depend upon God and His infinite goodness and power to take them safely to the desired haven in the life to come. They are becoming willing to trust God as the only one who cares and provides for their every need in this life. They are learning by obedient and voluntary surrender to the will of God in all things that their lives are being enriched and blessed with those things that are worthy of their own creative makeup. They are learning that the highest glory of the creature is to live for the good of all concerned and to worship and serve God in true humility and harmony.

We conclude, therefore, that there is a divine providence supplying the needs of all creation, but that the believers who surrender to God and conform to the Bible have a particular providence in their lives and that they should get in life all that sinners can and do get of the good things of life—plus an abundance of what sinners cannot hope to get until they surrender to God and conform to His will. No child of God, as a particular subject of special providence, should be without what sinners enjoy of material benefits, health, and happiness. They should have all these if they belong to God, for they are in the right position with God to get these things. Every Christian should be ashamed of himself and repent of his unbelief and lack of trust in God for these blessings. He should draw near to God and let God work out all these advantages in his life.

"All the promises of God in him are yea, and in him Amen, unto the glory of God . . . For all things are yours . . . And ye are Christ's; and Christ is God's" (2 Cor. 1:20; 1 Cor. 3:21-23).

Chapter Sixteen

EXERCISING UNLIMITED AUTHORITY OVER ALL SATANIC POWERS

If one wants to have power with God and exercise unlimited authority over all the powers of the devil he must first learn that such is possible and that it is the will of God according to the Bible. That such is promised in Scripture to every believer is clear from the following points:

Every Believer in Christ Should Have Power to:

1. *Overcome all sin and bad habits* (Mt. 1:21; Eph. 1:7; 2:1-9; 1 Jn. 1:7-9; 2:29; 3:5-10; 5:1-5, 18; Rom. 6:1-23; 8:1-13; Gal. 5:16-26).
2. *Cast out demons* (Mk. 16:17; Lk. 24:49; Jn. 14:12; Acts 1:8; 8:7; 16:18; 19:11-17; Rom. 15:18-19, 29; Heb. 2:3-4).
3. *Be immune from poisons and control wild beasts* (Mk. 1:13; 16:18; Lk. 10:19; Jn. 14:12; Acts 28:3-6; Ps. 91:1-16).
4. *Heal everyone prayed for* (Mt. 4:23-24; 8:16-17; 9:35; 12:15; 14:36; 21:14; Lk. 4:40; 6:19; 9:6; Jn. 14:12; Acts 2:43; 3:6; 4:10, 30, 33; 5:12-16; 6:3-8;

8:4-12; 9:34; 10:38; 11:21; 14:8-10, 19-20; 15:4, 12; 19:11-21; 28:1-10; Rom. 15:18-29; Heb. 2:3-4; Jas. 5:14-16).

5. *Raise the dead* (Jn. 11; 14:12; Acts 9:40; 20:9-10).

6. *Bind and loose anything* (Mt. 9:1-8; 16:18; 18:18; Jn. 14:12; 20:23).

7. *Destroy the works of Satan* (Jn. 14:12; 17:18; Acts 10:38; 1 Jn. 3:8; 4:17).

8. *Get everything prayed for* (Mt. 6:4-6, 18; 7:7-11; 17:20-21; 18:18-20; 21:21-22; Mk. 9:23; 11:22-24; Lk. 11:1-13; 18:1-18; Jn. 14:12-15; 15:7, 16; 16:23-26; Heb. 11:6; Jas. 1:5-8; 1 Jn. 3:21-22; 5:14-15; Ps. 91; Isa. 58).

9. *Control the elements and do all kinds of miracles* (Jn. 14:12; Lk. 24:49; 1 Cor. 12:1-11; 2 Tim. 2:21; Heb. 2:3-4; Mk. 16:15-20; Acts 1:8).

10. *Execute judgment* (Jn. 14:12; Acts 5:1-11; 13:6-12; 1 Cor. 4:21; 5:1-5).

11. *Get abundant provision for life* (Mt. 6:25-33; Mk. 11:22-24; Jn. 14:12-15; 15:7, 16; 16:23-26; 2 Cor. 9:8-11; Phil. 4:19; 3 Jn. 2).

12. *Exercise power over all the power of the devil* (Lk. 10:19; 24:49; Mk. 16:15-20; Jn. 14:12-15; 15:7; 16:23-26; Acts 1:8; 2 Cor. 10:4-5; Eph. 6:10-18).

13. *Have complete knowledge of the truth beyond all doubt* (Jn. 7:16-17; 8:31-32; 14:16-17, 26; 15:26-27; 16:7-15; 2 Tim. 2:15; 3:16-17).

14. *Have rivers of living waters flowing out of the innermost being* (Jn. 7:37-39; Acts 2:1-11, 38-39; 5:32; Eph. 5:18; Mt. 5:6).

15. *Have freedom from darkness into complete light* (Jn. 8:12, 31-32; Acts 26:18; 1 Jn. 1:7-9; 2 Cor. 3:18; Eph. 4:17-21; 5:8-16).

16. *Have power to do the works of Christ and even greater than He did* (Jn. 14:12-15; Lk. 24:49; Acts 1:8; Mk. 16:15-20; 1 Cor. 12:4-11; 2 Cor. 10:4-5).

17. *Have healing and sound health* (Jn. 14:12-15; 15:7, 16; 16:23-26; Mk. 9:23; 11:22-24; Rom. 8:11; 3 Jn. 2; Mt. 8:16-17; 1 Pet. 2:24; Heb. 11:6; Ps. 91; Isa. 58).

18. *The gifts of the Spirit* (1 Cor. 1:7; 12:4-11, 31; 14:1; Rom. 12:4-8).

19. *Impart the gifts to others* (Rom. 1:11; 1 Tim. 4:14; 2 Tim. 1:6; Heb. 6:2).

20. *Have the fruit of the Spirit* (Gal. 5:22-24).

21. *Get and impart the Spirit baptism to others* (Jn. 14:12; Acts 1:4-5; 2:1-39; 5:32; 8:17; 9:17; 10:44-48; 19:1-7; Heb. 6:2).

22. *Exercise unlimited authority in this life in all the fullness of God according to the Gospel* (Lk. 24:49; Jn. 14:12-15; 15:7, 16; Mk. 9:23; 11:22-24; 16:15-20; Mt. 17:20; 21:21-22; Acts 1:8; 2:38-39, 43; 3:6; 4:10-16, 29-33; 5:1-16; 6:3-8; 8:5-20; 9:17-18, 32:43; 11:21; 13:6-12; 14:3, 8-20, 27; 15:4, 12; 16:16-34; 19:1-20; 20:9-12; 28:1-10; Rom. 1:11; 15:18-19, 29; 1 Cor. 1:7, 18-24; 2:1-5; 4:19-21; 5:1-5; 9:18; 12:1-11, 28-31; 13:1-3; 14:1-40; 16:10; 2 Cor. 3:6-18; 4:7; 5:20; 6:7; 8:7; 10:3-11; 12:9, 12; 13:4, 10; Gal. 3:3-5, 14; Eph. 1:19-20; 6:10-18; Phil. 4:9; Col. 1:11; 2:10; 1 Th. 1:5; 2:13; 2 Th. 1:11; 2:17; 1 Tim. 4:14; 2 Tim. 1:6-8, 14; 2:21; 3:5; Titus 2:14; Heb. 2:3-4; 6:1-2; Jas. 2:18; 5:14-16; 2 Pet. 2:4; 3 Jn. 2; Jude 3, 20-24).

According to all the above–cited promises, and many other Scriptures, it can be seen that no believer is limited in obtaining for himself and others the provision for all his needs in this life and the life to come. The reason we have listed so many Scriptures to prove each point is that we want you to realize that God has made provision for you in every way and to show you that there are hundreds of Scriptures to prove our claims. The only thing that will hinder you from obtaining what you want is your unbelief. There is no excuse for unbelief in view of the abundant promises given in these Scriptures and in view of the fact that early believers (not only the apostles but many ordinary believers) experienced and enjoyed these blessings, as you can see by reading all the above passages.

Modern Believers Can Have All New Testament Experiences

If early believers actually experienced and enjoyed these blessings, why can't modern believers? Does not God still love us? Does He not have the same power today? Do we not need these benefits today as in the first century? Are the promises still the same? Has God changed His program? Has He withdrawn His promises? Has He ceased to make provision for men today as He made in days gone by? Is He a respecter of persons? Where in Scripture does it say that these things are not for us today? Where does it say that God has changed His mind and has done away with His provision for all men who will dare believe?

There is not one hint in the Bible that God has done away with the blessings of the early believers. This is a theory of modern unbelieving men who would rather manufacture doctrines of unbelief to excuse their own weakness and lack of power than to face the plain facts and put forth some effort to meet the conditions that will enable them to attain to these benefits.

Only Rebels and Unbelievers Deny Truth

A man would have to be an unbeliever and a determined rebel against God and His Word to deny that man can get what he wants from God. If you want to take the side of those who reject God and His Word, then don't complain because you are not receiving all the good things in life to enjoy. Don't complain because God never seems to answer your prayers. Don't complain if God's Word is not being fulfilled in you. God will not help you when you refuse help. He will not force you to be blessed against your will. You are a free moral agent, and God respects the sovereignty of your free choice. He expects you to use common intelligence and cooperate with Him instead of His enemies if you want the benefits for which Christ died and which He has abundantly promised to those that will love and obey Him.

Your Personal Responsibility

Quit associating with unbelievers though they belong to your church—even though some are your spiritual leaders and advisers. You cannot afford to take such advice that will rob you of the riches of life in the gospel. Begin to look around for people of like faith. If you cannot find any in your community, then make some by getting these truths to your neighbors. Soon you will have friends who will believe God with you, and together you can study and pray and reap the blessings that are yours. All you need to do is to follow the instructions which you can plainly see in your own Bible as we give them to you.

Demon Powers Must Be Defeated

Satanic powers must be defeated if one wants the unlimited blessings of the Gospel that we have listed above. These benefits are for all men and they will be fully realized when complete victory over Satan is gained through Christ, the Holy Spirit, and the Word of God. All the blessings listed above will be fully realized when complete victory over demon powers is accomplished.

Weapons of Spiritual Warfare are Provided

There are several Scriptures that make clear what the spiritual weapons are and how to use them in gaining victory over sin and Satan. The weapons of our warfare are referred to as not being carnal or natural, but spiritual: "For though we walk in the flesh, we do not war after the flesh: (For the weapons of our warfare are not carnal, but mighty through God to the pulling down of strong holds;) Casting down imaginations and every high thing that exalteth itself against the knowledge of God, and bringing into captivity every thought to the obedience of Christ" (2 Cor. 10:3-5).

217

This passage certainly teaches complete victory over all the powers of darkness, even to the point that every thought is brought down to the obedience of Christ. If there is such a possibility, then Christians should learn about it and cooperate with God until full victory is attained in Christ through the Gospel. We do not have to pray, "If it be thy will grant complete victory over Satan," for it is clear that it is God's will, and that He has provided full means for spiritual warfare and complete victory in life over all things that exalt themselves against God and His people.

In Ephesians 6:10-18, the Apostle Paul gives us a description of the whole armour of God, which Christians are commanded to wear in order to stand against the wiles of the devil. "For we wrestle not against flesh and blood, but against principalities, against powers, against the rulers of darkness of this world, against spiritual wickedness in high places. Wherefore take unto you the whole armour of God, that ye may be able to withstand in the evil day, and having done all, to stand" (Eph. 6:10-18).

The study of such Scriptures, as well as the subject of spiritual warfare, are foreign doctrines to today's average church member. Many of our Christian leaders are either completely ignorant of such things or, even worse, are hostile to these clear teachings of Scripture. They teach a social, shallow, and worldly gospel that would not cause a single demon to blink an eye. Many of them scoff at such things, classing as relics of the past the ideas of the reality of Satan, demonic forces, and spiritual warfare. Christians are being taught that there is no such thing as a victorious life in Christ and victory over sins and bad habits; that there is no wrong in worldly pleasures; and that there is no need to be so strict in living a Christian life.

The whole armour of God is still needful, and real warfare against demons is just as real as it ever was. The armour of God in Ephesians 6:10-18 is listed as follows: "Stand therefore, having your loins girt about with truth, and having on the breastplate of righteousness; And your feet shod with the preparation of the gospel of peace; Above all, taking the shield of faith, wherewith ye shall be able to quench all the fiery darts of the wicked. And take the helmet of salvation, and the sword of the Spirit, which is the word of God: Praying always with all prayer and supplication in the Spirit, and watching thereunto with all perseverance and supplication for all saints" (Eph:6:14-18).

This armour of God is made up of seven parts: three for enduement of power—the girdle, the breastplate, and the shoes; two for weapons of defense—the shield of faith and the helmet of salvation; and two for offence— the sword of the Spirit, which is the Word of God, and prayer in the Spirit.

Spiritual Qualifications Necessary

The use of this armour presupposes the reality of the new birth and personal knowledge of sonship with God and baptism in the Holy Spirit or the enduement of power from on High.

With such equipment for spiritual warfare it is impossible to be defeated by the devil. It is impossible for one to live in helplessness and weakness in his spiritual life. It is noticeable that this whole armour centers around the Holy Spirit, the Word of God, the personal experience of the new birth, a holy life, walking in the light of truth, trusting in God for deliverance and protection, and aggressive warfare in prayer against the forces of darkness.

One must learn to use the Word of God against the devil, just as Jesus did in gaining full mastery over him (Mt. 4:1-11). One must learn to refuse all temptations, to abide in Christ and to have God's Word abiding in him, control self, live a godly life—one that is consecrated to the total will of God. One must be an overcomer, face the world and demonic powers in all boldness in the Spirit, live and walk in the Spirit, and pray with unwavering faith and confidence in God. Anyone who will do this will become a complete master of himself as well as of all the demonic powers that constantly war on God's children.

One must become baptized in the Holy Spirit, just like Christ and the early disciples were. The baptism in the Spirit is the enduement of power for service (Lk. 24:49; Acts 1:8), the complete anointing of the Spirit in the life of a believer (Isa. 11:1-2; 42:1-5; 61:1-3; Mt. 3:11, 16-17; Lk. 4:16-21; Jn. 3:34; Acts 10:38), and the immersion of the child of God in all the fullness of God (Jn. 7:37-39; 14:12, 16-17, 26; 15:26; 16:13-15; Acts 1:4-8; 2:1-47; 3:6; 8:12-20; 9:17; 10:44-48; 19:1-7; Rom. 15:18-19, 29; Eph. 3:19; 5:18).

The way to receive such a baptism is to "ask" the Heavenly Father (Lk. 11:13), believe for the full anointing of the Spirit and the enduement of power and yield to the Spirit until the works of God are manifest in your life (Jn. 7:37-39; Lk. 24:49; Acts 2:38-39; 5:32; Rom. 12:1-2; Eph. 3:14-20). The list of benefits that were outlined in Point 1 are the evidences of the fullness of God. Do not be satisfied until every one of these evidences are personal realities. Do not accept only one of these benefits as the fullness of God. Until all of them are real experiences, no person is filled with *all* the fullness of God.

The fullness of God naturally includes any measure of the Spirit anyone ever has received. It literally means that one will have power to do the works of Christ and even greater works than what He did (Jn. 14:12). It means that one will experience all the gifts and fruit of the Spirit like Christ and the apostles. It means exactly as we have stated in Point 1 above, that one living in all the fullness of God will be able to do any and all of the things we have listed from Scripture that were the normal experiences of the early church.

A Warning to All

To have power to exercise unlimited authority in the fullness of God means that you do not reject any part of the Bible or be ashamed of any experience that God gave to early believers. It matters not what men condemn and make fun of; it matters not how unpopular it may be; and it matters not whether or not it is accepted by all churches, the fact remains that the above–mentioned experiences are on record so that every honest person can see for himself that early disciples had these blessings. No man has to be deceived (or be tempted to think that he might receive a wrong spirit or mani-festation) if he will follow the instructions outlined in Chapter Three.

The fact remains that every person, if he is the least bit honest, can read the above passages for himself if he has doubts about what we say. He will have to acknowledge that such blessings were present in the lives of early Christians. He must then conclude that they are for believers today, just as much as they were for the first Christians, or the Scriptures are not true. He must further conclude that if he wants such bless-ings he must accept them and get them exactly like the early Christians did. If he does not want them, then let him be satisfied with a powerless and helpless life when he comes to face the devil and evil spirit forces; when he comes to heal the sick; and when he needs to do the works of Christ that every believer is supposed to have power to do (Jn. 14:12).

Promises of Unlimited Power in God

Whether it be asking God for salvation from sin, heal-ing for the body, the spiritual gifts or any of life's needs, there are certain principles given in Scripture that must be followed before one can get what he wants. We have searched the Gospels to find what God requires of men in order to get power with God in prayer and have defi-nite authority over demons. Be sure that you understand the requirements of God and what is promised when one meets these conditions. The promises of God in these passages are printed in italics and the conditions in standard type. Note the requirement, and then the promise in each passage. The requirements of God and His unlimited promises of power are recorded in many Scriptures, as follows:

1. "Ask, and *it shall be given you*; seek, and *ye shall find*: knock, and *it shall be opened unto you*" (Mt. 7:7-11).
2. "Believe ye that I am able to do this? . . . According to your faith *be it unto you*" (Mt. 9:28-29).
3. "If ye have faith as a grain of mustard seed . . . *nothing shall be impossible unto you*" (Mt. 17:20-21).
4. "If two of you shall agree on earth as touching anything that they shall ask . . . *it shall be done*" (Mt. 18:19).
5. "If ye have faith, and doubt not . . . *it shall be done. And all things, whatsoever ye shall ask in prayer, believing, ye shall receive*" (Mt. 21:21-22).
6. If thou canst believe, *all things are possible to him that believeth*" (Mk. 9:23).
7. "Have faith in God . . . and shall not doubt in his heart, but shall believe that those things which he saith shall come to pass; *he shall have whatsoever he saith* . . . What things soever ye desire, when ye pray, believe that ye receive them, *and ye shall have them.* And when ye stand praying, forgive, if ye have ought against any: *that your father also . . . may forgive you your tresspasses.* But if ye do not forgive, neither will your father which is in heaven forgive your trespasses" (Mk. 11:22-26).
8. "And these *signs shall follow them that believe*; In my name *shall they cast out devils; they shall speak with new tongues: they shall take up* (Greek, *airo*, "to remove," "take out of the way," "destroy," "put

away," as in Jn. 1:29; 15:2; 19:15; 1 Cor. 5:2; 1 Jn. 3:5; Mt. 22:13; Acts 21:36; 22:22) *serpents: and if they shall drink any deadly thing it shall not hurt them; they shall lay hands on the sick, and they shall recover"* (Mk. 16:15-20).

9. "Because of his importunity *he will arise and give him as many as he needeth . . . how much more shall your heavenly father give the holy spirit to them that ask him"* (Lk. 11:5-13).

10. "Men ought always to pray, and not to faint [lose heart] . . . Because this widow troubleth me, *I will avenge her,* lest by her continued coming she weary [pester] me . . . And *shall not god avenge his own elect, which cry day and night unto him,* though he bear long with them? I tell you *he will avenge them speedily"* (Lk. 18:1-8).

11. "Whosoever believeth in him *should not perish, but have everlasting life . . .* He that believeth on the Son *hath everlasting life"* (Jn. 3:16, 36).

12. "If any man thirst, let him come unto me and drink. He that believeth on me, as the Scripture hath said, *out of his belly shall flow rivers of living water.* (But this spake he of the Spirit, *which they that believe on him should receive"* (Jn. 7:37-39; Mt. 5:6).

13. "If ye continue in my word, *then are ye my disciples indeed; and ye shall know the truth, and the truth shall make you free . . .* If the Son therefore shall make you free, *ye shall be free indeed"* (Jn. 8:31-36).

14. "If any man serve me, *him will my father honour"* (Jn. 12:25-26).

15. "He that believeth on me, *the works that I do shall he do also; and greater works than these shall he do;* because I go to my Father. And whatsoever ye shall

ask in my name, *that will I do*, that the Father may be glorified in the Son. If ye shall ask any thing in my name, *I will do it*" (Jn. 14:12-15).

16. "If ye abide in me, and my words abide in you, *ye shall ask what ye will and it shall be done unto you . . . If ye keep my* commandments, *ye shall abide in my love* . . . . Ye have not chosen me, but I have chosen you, and ordained you, *that ye should go and bring forth fruit, and that your fruit should remain: that whatsoever ye shall ask of the father in my name, he may give it you*" (Jn. 15:7, 10, 16).

17. "*I send the promise of my father upon you*: but tarry ye in the city of Jerusalem, *until ye be endued with power from on high*" (Lk. 24:49; Jn. 14:16-17, 26; 15:26; 16:13-15; Acts 1:4-8).

18. "Whatsoever ye shall ask the Father in my name, *he will give it you* . . . ask, *and ye shall receive,* that your joy may be full" (Jn. 16:23-26).

19. "Repent, and be baptized . . . And *ye shall receive the gift of the holy ghost. for the promise is unto you, and to your children, and to all that are afar off, even as many as the lord our god shall call*" (Acts 2:38-39). "We are witnesses of these things; and so is also the Holy Ghost, *whom god has given to them that obey him*" (Acts 5:32).

20. Now concerning spiritual gifts, brethren, I would not have you to be ignorant . . . Now there are diversities of gifts, but the same Spirit. And there are differences of administrations, but the same Lord. And there are diversities of operations, but it is the same God which worketh all in all. But the manifestation of the Spirit is given to *every man* to profit withal. *for to one is given* by the Spirit the word of wisdom; *to*

another the word of knowledge by the same Spirit; *to another* faith by the same Spirit; *to another* the gifts of healing by the same Spirit; *to another* the working of miracles; *to another* prophecy; *to another* discerning of spirits; *to another* divers kinds of tongues; *to another* the interpretation of tongues: But all these worketh the selfsame spirit, *dividing to every man severally as he will* . . . But *covet earnestly the best gifts* . . . Follow after charity, and *desire spiritual gifts*" (1 Cor. 12:1-11, 31; 14:1; Rom.12:3-8; 15:18-19, 29; Eph. 3:19).

21. "But without faith it is impossible to please him: for he that cometh to God must believe that he is, and *that he is a rewarder of them that diligently seek him*" (Heb. 11:6).

22. "If any man lack wisdom, let him ask of God, *that giveth to all men liberally, and upbraideth not: and it shall be given him.* But let him ask in faith, nothing wavering. For he that wavereth is like the wave of the sea driven with the wind and tossed. *for let not that man think that he shall receive any thing of the lord*" (Jas. 1:5-8).

23. "God resisteth the proud, *but giveth grace to the humble.* Submit yourselves therefore to God. Resist the devil, *and he will flee from you.* Draw nigh to God, *and he will draw nigh to you.* Cleanse your hands. ye sinners; and purify your hearts, ye double minded . . . humble yourselves in the sight of the Lord, and *he shall lift you up*" (Jas. 4:6-10).

24. "My little children, let us not love in word, neither in tongue; but in deed and in truth . . . For if our heart condemn us, God is greater than our heart, and knoweth all things. Beloved, if our heart condemn

us not, *then have we confidence toward god. and whatsoever we ask, we receive of him*, because we keep his commandments, and do those things that are pleasing in his sight" (1 Jn. 3:18-24).

25. "And this is the confidence that we have in him, that, if we ask any thing according to his will, *he heareth us*: And if we know that he hear us, *whatsoever we ask, we know that we have the petitions that we desired of him*" (1 Jn. 5:14-15).

The Secret of Power with God

The secret of power with God is to believe His Word and conform to it to the letter. This means that one must be born again and must be filled with all the fullness of God and work for God upon the authority of the principles stated in the Scriptures above. The secret of power with God is God Himself in the life of a believer, working in and through him to will and to do of His own pleasure (2 Cor. 4:7; 10:4-5; Eph. 3:19-20; 6:10-18; Phil. 2:13-16; 2 Tim. 2:15-21). One must become endued with power from on High by doing what the above passages teach. He must receive the gifts of the Holy Spirit and through the Spirit master himself and all demonic powers. He must learn how to pray and exercise unwavering faith in God and in His Word. He must learn to resist the devil and defeat him through the Spirit of God and the Word of God (Eph. 6:10-18; 2 Cor. 10:4-6).

Complete Mastery over the Devil Possible

One must not only believe that complete mastery over the devil is possible and that it is the will of God, but he must act in harmony with God and His Word to make it a reality in his life. The above promises reveal the conditions one must meet. They also state the divine promises of power to receive complete victory over the devil and all evil. There is no question about faith, prayer, and power that cannot be answered by the above Scriptures. God cannot lie. The devil is the liar when he tells you that you cannot become his master. He is already a defeated foe. You are already the victor over him in Christ if you will take your rightful place in the Gospel against Him. You do not have to fear the devil in the least. He cannot stand before the power of the name of Jesus and faith in the blood of Jesus. He knows that Jesus is His master and that you are also his master through faith in the name and blood of Jesus Christ. Rebuke the devil and demons by using the name of Jesus, their master, and by pleading the merits of the power of that name over them, through faith in the atonement. Demons cannot stand before you. Sicknesses will have to go. Pains will have to leave. Sins and demonic forces behind bad habits will have to depart. Demons that hinder and cause unbelief and doubt will loose their hold on you if you resist them and refuse to obey them. Every failure and spiritual defeat will be a thing of the past. Financial problems can be solved by taking a firm stand against these powers. God will back up His promises and will grant everything that is asked in faith in the name of Jesus.

How to Deal with Demons

If doubt, unbelief, pain, sickness, poverty, unanswered prayer, lack of spiritual power, or anything else that is contrary to the Word of God, continues to linger and you begin to wonder what is wrong, simply rebuke demons in the name of Jesus and claim the fulfillment of the promises of God for what you want. For example, you are promised that if you do not doubt you will get whatever you want. Therefore, resist doubt and say, "You demon of doubt and unbelief, I rebuke you in the name of Jesus Christ your master, whom you fear and whom you cannot stand before. Get out. I refuse to tolerate you any longer. I have victory over you now through faith in the blood of Christ and the name of Jesus Christ." In other words, talk to the devil as you would to any other enemy. Resist him just as you would any other person that is trying to rob you—the devil desires to rob you of the benefits for which Christ died. What have you to fear from the devil, fallen angels, demons, or fallen men? Refuse to tolerate doubt and unbelief. Believe that what you asked for is already accomplished. Count it done and act as if the prayer was already answered. Give thanks to God for the answer. Refuse to take "no" for an answer. Refuse even to think that it is possible that you have not been heard of God. Do not give place to the devil (Eph. 4:27).

If you have a pain, rebuke it and the demon by its name, and command the demon of pain to be gone. If your are experiencing sickness, rebuke the demon of sickness and cast it out in the name of Jesus. If it is some temptation that is plaguing you, rebuke the tempting devil and refuse to yield to sin or any bad habit. Call the demon of sin by name and deal with it as with a person, for all demons are persons. If it is the habit of smoking, rebuke the demon of nicotine and claim power over it by faith in the blood of Christ to cleanse the very desire out of your life. Claim that the nicotine devil must leave your bloodstream and not bother you again. If it is some financial problem, rebuke the poverty devils and claim the answer to prayer. What ever the trouble is, deal with that particular thing as being of the devil. You have the name of Jesus and you have faith in God, in His Word, and in the blood of Christ. You have the blessed Holy Spirit to help you; that is, if you are a child of God and are baptized in the Spirit. You even have the Holy Spirit in a measure when born again (Rom. 8:9-16). You know God if you are His child. You know how to pray. You have Christian brethren to pray with you and for you. You have every means of grace and power to overcome Satan and all His work in your life, so use them to your best interests.

Use God's Own Affirmations

Take the many passages in the twenty–five references in Point 9 above and affirm everything that God has said. You do not have to listen to what men say, what the devil says, or what anyone else says. You have what God says and that is sufficient. Regardless of how impossible it seems for you to get what you want, you can still affirm what God says and it will increase your faith and bring about the seemingly impossible (Rom. 10:17). You can affirm with all assurance that the devil is a liar and God is true to His Word. You can quote and affirm what God says and refuse to quote what the devil or men say. You can maintain faith in spite of doubt and unbelief. You can claim victory in the face of men and devils and say, "It shall be done." How do you know it shall be done? Because God said so. Faith comes by hearing and hearing by the Word of God (Rom. 10:17).

You have the Word of God, so believe it. You can use one or all of the words of God in His promises. If you have met the requirements of the promises, you can claim their fulfillment in the face of seeming defeat. This is your duty. It is your obligation to God and He will see you through. If there is the slightest doubt that it might not work, you can still affirm what God says and go down fighting. God says you will not get what you want if you waver, so you have nothing to lose by doing what God says, even if you do not receive by having faith in His promises. However, there can be no defeat when you have faith, so dismiss even the very thought of defeat. Constantly affirm the following short and definite statements that are found in the promises referred to above.

God says, *"it shall be given you . . . ye shall find . . . it shall be opened unto you . . . how much more shall your heavenly father give good things to them that ask him"* (Mt. 7:7-11); *"nothing shall be impossible unto you"* (Mt. 17:20-21); *"it shall be done"* and *"ye shall receive"* (Mt. 18:19; 21-21-22); *"all things are possible to him that believeth"* (Mk. 9:23); *"he shall have whatsoever he saith . . . ye shall have them"* (Mk. 11:22-24); *"these signs shall follow them that believe"* (Mk. 16:15-20); *"ye shall know the truth, and the truth shall make you free"* (Jn. 8:31-36); *"him will my father honour"* (Jn. 12:25-26); *"the works that I do shall he do also . . . that will I do . . . I will do it"* (Jn. 14:12-15); *"ye shall ask what ye will and it shall be done unto you . . . whatsoever ye shall ask of the father in my name, he may give it you"* (Jn. 15:7, 16); *"he will give it you . . . ye shall receive"* (Jn. 16:23-26); *"he is a rewarder of them that diligently seek him"* (Heb. 11:6); *"giveth to all men liberally, and upbraideth not: and it shall be given him"* (Jas. 1:4-8); "HE [the devil] *shall flee from you! . . . he* [God] *will draw nigh to you . . . he shall lift you up"* (Jas. 4:6-10); *"whatsoever we ask we receive of him . . . he heareth us . . . we know that we have the petitions that we desired of him"* (1 Jn. 3:18-24; 5:14-15).

Be Sure Conditions Are Met

If one wants to fully experience all the benefits of God's promises, he must meet all the conditions laid down in connection with them. The quotations that were listed in the pervious section emphasize the "promise" part of certain Scriptures and the following quotations from the same passages emphasize the conditions one must meet in order to claim the blessings that are promised to all children of God:

(1) *Ask, seek,* and *knock* are the conditions of Matthew 7:7-11 if one wants to *receive, find,* and have the door *opened* to him.

(2) *Believe, have faith,* and *doubt not* are the conditions of Matthew 9:28-29; 17:20-21; 21:21-22; Mark 9:23; 16:15-20; etc.

(3) *Two persons must agree* that God will answer prayer is the requirement of Matthew 18:19.

(4) *Have faith in God, forgive others, doubt not in his heart, believe that those things which He saith shall come to pass, desire, pray, and believe that he receives them* are the conditions of Mark 11:22-26.

(5) *Because of his importunity, always pray and not lose heart,* and *cry day and night* unto God are the conditions of Luke 11:5-13; 18:1-8.

(6) *Thirst, come unto Me and drink,* and *believe on Me as the Scripture hath said* are the conditions of John 7:37-39; 14:12-15. To believe "as the Scripture hath said" means that there is not the slightest doubt or wavering as to the answer (Hab. 2:4; Isa. 53:1; Jas. 1:5-8).

(7) *If ye continue in my word* and *if any man will serve Me* are the conditions of John 8:31-36; 12:25-26.

(8) *Ask in My name, if ye abide in Me and My words abide in you,* and *keep My commandments* are the requirements listed in John 14:12-15; 15:7, 10, 16; 16:23-26.

(9) *Tarry ye in the city of Jerusalem* or *wait for the promise of the Father until ye be endued with power from on high* is the requirement in Luke 24:49; John 14:16-17, 26; 15:26; 16:13-15; Acts 1:4-8. This simply means that, since the Holy Spirit has come, that we ask God and yield to the Spirit for the fullness of God until it is actually manifest in our lives just as it was in the lives of the early disciples (Mt. 28:19-20; Mk. 16:15-20; Acts 2:38-39; 5:32; Lk. 11:13; Eph. 1:18-19; 3:16-20; 5:18).

(10) *Repent, be baptized,* and *obey* are the conditions of Acts 2:38-39; 5:32, providing one wants the Holy Spirit baptism.

(11) *Be not ignorant* of spiritual gifts and *covet* and *desire* them are the conditions which must be met in order to receive them, according to the Apostle Paul's letters to the churches in Corinth and Rome (1 Corinthians 12:1-31; 14:1-40; Romans 12:3-8).

(12) *One must believe* that God is and that He is a rewarder of them that diligently seek Him if one truly desires to receive answers to prayer (Heb. 11:6).

(13) *Ask in faith, nothing wavering* is the condition of getting every prayer answered, according to James 1:5-8.

(14) *Be humble, submit to God*, and *resist the devil* are other conditions of answered prayer (Jas. 4:6-10).

(15) *Love in word, not in tongue* and *if our heart condemn us not* are the requirements of 1 John 3:18-24.

(16) *Ask according to the will of God* is the final requirement of John if we expect answers to all prayers (1 Jn. 5:14-15). This means that we pray for those things promised by God and that are in harmony with His Word.

One should memorize both the conditions and the benefits of the promises and affirm both at all times when seeking an answer to prayer. He should intelligently refuse to be denied until he receives the answer and then be thankful to God for it. By the exercise of the gifts of the Spirit, the full anointing of the Spirit, and power with God in prayer, one will be able to have absolute authority over all demonic and satanic powers.

No Defeat Possible to Christians

If God said these things, they are true and they are "yea and amen to them that believe" (2 Cor. 1:20). If they are true, they cannot be lies. If they are not lies then it is impossible for any child of God to pray in faith and not receive. These statements should be used against the devils and men who seek to discourage us in prayer. God says if we will use the sword of the Spirit, which is the Word of God, that we shall be able to quench all the fiery darts of the wicked one (Eph. 6:10-18). No man has a right to affirm that God is not true and that He will not keep His Word, so the way of complete victory over the devil and his agents becomes clear to every saint who will obey God and His Word.

FINIS

Printed in the USA
CPSIA information can be obtained
at www.ICGtesting.com
LVHW052256110124
768815LV00037B/387

9 781558 290662